6/16

HOME
THE
CHILDREN

THE HOME CHILDREN

THEIR PERSONAL STORIES

EDITED BY PHYLLIS HARRISON

J. GORDON SHILLINGFORD
PUBLISHING INC

The Home Children
Their Personal Stories

Phyllis Harrison, Editor

@ 1979, Phyllis Harrison
First printing, March 1979
New Format Edition, October 2003

Book design by Gallant Design Ltd.
Printed and bound in Canada.

We acknowledge the financial assistance of The Canada Council for
the Arts and the Manitoba Arts Council for our publishing program.

National Library of Canada Cataloguing in Publication

The home children: their personal stories / Phyllis Harrison, editor.

Includes index.
ISBN 0-920486-15-0

      1. Socially handicapped children--Canada--Biography. 2.
Socially handicapped children--Great Britain--Biography. 3. Foster
home care--Canada. 4. Children--Employment--Canada. I. Harrison,
Phyllis, 1918-

HV887.C3H65 2003   362.7'3'0922   C2003-905368-7

*To the Home Children and to the Homes that
sought to put hope into deprived lives*

ACKNOWLEDGMENTS

When one undertakes to research and write the story of an event in Canada's development, it cannot be done without the contributions of a great many people. I regret that I cannot mention by name the hundreds who either contributed to the work, or who sustained me with their enthusiasm during the past 10 years. However, I first want to acknowledge the enormous contribution made by the men and women who were once part of the British Child Emigration Movement, and whose stories in this book make this of Canadian history one of the most poignant. They have written their stories simply and well, sharing their childhood experiences with all of us.

In the United Kingdom I profited from the help of several of the Children's Homes who gave me access to records and pictures. Of special mention are the Barnardo Homes, the Church of England Children's Bureau, the National Children's Home, Fegan Home, and Middlemore Home. I am particularly indebted to Quarrier Homes of Scotland for their hospitality to me.

Closer to home I acknowledge the help of the staff of the Public Archives of Canada. I especially want to thank archivists Ian McClymont and Doug Whyte.

My special thanks go to my friends Mildred Flanagan and Marjorie McLean who voluntarily sorted letters and catalogued them. I also appreciate the assistance of Doris Roy who addressed hundreds of envelopes.

Finally, I would like to thank the 40 Canadian newspapers and the Legion Magazine for printing my letter indicating my search for former Home Children. Without their co-operation I might never have found the Canadians and Americans whose stories are in this book—stories which, in another decade, would well have been lost to Canada.

CONTENTS

CONTENTS

CONTENTS

PREFACE

The 'Home' children, thousands of them, were sent to a young, struggling, harsh, pioneering Canada—mostly rural and rough. They were, and still are, a major factor in the Canadian story, measured in part by their more than one million descendants across the country. Orphans, waifs and strays—they poured into the new land. Some were profoundly fortunate in their destination and destiny. Others met harsh exploitation and bitterness.

They came—were sent—in a mixture of intense confusion, terror, child courage and, occasionally, optimism. They absorbed the shock of early Canada, cultural and geographical; lived a grinding pioneer life we can now barely comprehend; fought, died, and survived the holocaust of trench warfare; struggled through the Depression and in turn, watched their own children enter another war. Each of these children presents a struggle to make a life and, in the process, to add a piece in the building of a country.

The epic of the 'Home' children in Canada had been almost totally ignored until Phyllis Harrison began her research. The letters published here, and some will find their contents incredible, show defenceless orphans who were despised and exploited in Canada's mean colonial world where anti-English prejudices flourished—and still linger. One must remember, however, when reflecting on bitter experiences, what worse lives these boys and girls could have expected had they remained in the industrial slums of Great Britain. In Canada a few of these children found good homes and many finally achieved a fuller and better life.

Their lives and thinking contrasts with the current Canadian mood of self-pity and dependence, and this brings me to Phyllis Harrison's inordinate humane knowledge of the 'Home' children. The first time we met, she described their ethos in terms of the old virtues: hard work, honesty, self-reliance, and a devotion to family. My father came to Canada at 11, a 'Home' boy from Frodsham, and knowing only that, she went on to describe him with uncanny accuracy. Next, with a disarming smile, she described me with a like candor and precision.

Through these letters in The Home Children, you meet these immigrant children, gain insights into Canada as it was then, and find some other perceptions of Canada as it is now.

William E. Taylor, Jr.
Director, National Museum of Man
National Museums of Canada, Ottawa

INTRODUCTION

In this 20th century of citizen's rights and state responsibility it is difficult to believe that the experiences of Oliver Twist are not far behind us. There are many Canadians who, in childhood, experienced some of the same hardships, the same exploitation, and the same necessity to survive in a fairly hostile world.

These men and women, known in their early years as 'Home Children', were rescued from similar harsh conditions and placed in philanthropic Homes in the United Kingdom. Often, they were orphans; others had parents who, for reasons of poverty, illness or sheer inability to cope with life's problems, had relinquished their sons and daughters to be raised in the Homes. In the 1860s these children became the object of a philanthropic movement to improve their chances in life. One of the options offered to them was emigration to Canada.

Nineteenth-century Britain was the most powerful and the wealthiest nation in the world. At the same time, the industrial advancement of technology in that century meant that machines replaced human skill and effort. Nonetheless, the lure of factory jobs created by the industrial revolution caused a migration from the country to the city, and slums grew in London and other industrial cities in Great Britain. Since poverty was viewed as the responsibility of its victims, minimal provision was made by the state for jobless men or women and their families. They could go into the workhouse, try to eke out a living as a pedlar, or go 'into service'. There was no universal provision for educating children in England until 1870 and no compulsory education until 10 years later. Vast numbers of children lived on the streets surviving largely by their wits. Many died of hunger, exposure and sickness.

It was under these conditions that the British Child Emigration Movement began on October 28, 1869, when an English woman, Maria Susan Rye, boarded the Hibernian for Canada with 68 children gathered up from the workhouses and the streets of London, and the Kirkdale Industrial School of Liverpool.

Miss Rye conceived the idea of taking such children to Canada and placing them with farmers who, in return for what help the children could provide, promised to treat them like members of the family. The youngest of the children, those nine years or less, were considered placed for adoption, although there were no laws governing such contracts until the 1920s. Children 10 years of age and older were indentured to farmers to the ages of 16, 18 or 21 years, depending on the laws of the provinces.

Miss Rye's scheme included the establishment of a distributing centre in Canada for the children's reception and from which a modicum of supervision of their placement was provided. Her example was soon followed in 1870 by Annie Parlane Macpherson. Miss Macpherson was born near Campsie, Scotland, but had been involved in philanthropic work in London since 1861. During the 1870s, the movement grew to include children sent to Canada by Dr T. Bowman Stephenson, founder of the National Children's Home and Orphanage of London; John T. Middlemore of Birmingham; and the Orphans' Homes of Scotland founded near Glasgow by William Quarrier. By 1889 the Canadian Department of Agriculture, which was responsible for immigration, recorded more than 50 agents or agencies involved in bringing children to Canada for farm labour. Only three of these can be ranked as important philanthropic organizations: The Church of England Waifs and Strays Society, founded by the Reverend Edward de Montjoi Rudolf; Fegan Homes of Southwark, London, founded by J.W.C. Fegan; and the largest of all, the Barnardo Homes founded by Dr Thomas J. Barnardo. Before his death in 1905 at the age of 60, Dr Barnardo had established a network of children's Homes throughout the British Isles. By the turn of the 20th century, almost every second immigrant child in Canada was from a Barnardo Home.

All of these Homes had been established (with the exception of the Church of England Homes) by men and women who were motivated by strong religious convictions of an evangelical, fundamental, Protestant nature. There was also a Roman Catholic child emigration movement—first from Liverpool, founded by a Father Nugent and later from London under the sponsorship of Cardinal Henry Edward Manning. There were no Catholic distributing Homes in Canada until New Orpington Lodge,

Ottawa, opened in 1895 and Miss Brennan's Home for Catholic children opened in Montreal in 1897. The Great Depression of the 1930s ended the demand for child labourers in Canada, but up until that time, by official reckoning, nearly 100,000 children had crossed the Atlantic to find an opportunity in Canada.

The majority of the children were placed in Ontario; Roman Catholic children were generally sent to Quebec. Nova Scotia and New Brunswick received children from the Liverpool Sheltering Homes founded by Annie Macpherson's sister Louisa Birt. This territory, however, was taken over by the Middlemore Homes in the 1890s and Fairview, a Middlemore distributing Home, opened in Halifax in 1897.

Dr Barnardo was a leader in exploring opportunities for children in the western provinces after the railway reached Manitoba in 1881. He had a Home for boys in Winnipeg and a training farm at Russell, Manitoba, for older boys. In Ontario there were Barnardo Homes in Peterborough and Toronto; a Fegan Home in Toronto; a Stephenson Home in Hamilton; a Quarrier Home 'for Scotch children' in Brockville; and Macpherson Homes in Belleville, Stratford and Guelph and in Knowlton, Quebec. The original Canadian Home was opened by Maria Rye in 1869 at Niagara-on-the-Lake; after 1900 there were many other Homes.

My search for information on the British Child Emigration Movement, which has resulted in this book, The Home Children, began in 1968. I had noted references to these immigrant children in an earlier research project undertaken for the Children's Aid Society in Ottawa. Who were these children, why had they been brought to Canada, and were any of them still living?

In Belleville, while seeking information on the Marchmont Macpherson Home founded in 1870, I interviewed Miss Nellie Merry, a descendant of Annie Macpherson's sister, Mrs Rachel Merry. Miss Merry, a retired school teacher then in her 79th year, had spent her childhood in these Homes. Her grandparents lived in Canada as superintendents of both the Stratford and Marchmont Homes. From her I learned that the Marchmont records had been sent back to England when Marchmont Home was closed. In 1925 the Macpherson-Birt organizations had been amalgamated with Barnardo Homes and all the records transferred to the Barnardo Homes at Barkingside, Ilford, Essex.

In 1969 I visited the Barnardo Homes where everything, except the new administration building, looked exactly like the sketches in annual reports from the 1880s. Immaculate gardens and attractive cottages with climbing roses conjured up visions of small girls in pinafores. But one was abruptly brought back to the present by the happy shouts of girls and boys—many of them black children of West Indian background—dressed in jeans and jerseys.

A statue of Dr Thomas J. Barnardo, its great size indicative of the respect he still commands, stands within sound of the children's laughter. While the village is for homeless children, none will be sent off alone to make a new life in Canada. Still the largest private child-caring agency in Britain, the Barnardo Homes have adjusted to modern ideas and understanding of children's needs. A large staff strives to fulfil that policy set down so long ago by Dr Barnardo: 'No Destitute Child Ever Refused Admission'.

The Quarrier Village of Bridge-of-Weir, Scotland, was also visited. As I arrived a large bus had just discharged a group of garrulous women—the cleaning staff. This is perhaps the first change that former boys and girls returning to the village for a visit would notice. It is years since the children were expected to do the cleaning around the cottages which were their homes. Nor do they crawl into cold beds in unheated rooms; central heating was installed a number of years ago. There are other changes: mischievous children are no longer punished with a strap and the meals are the responsibility of individual cottage parents and vary with each unit. Former boys and girls recall the regulation 'orphanage' meals of porridge for breakfast, soup or stew at most other meals.

To facilitate my research a desk was provided in the administration building which had been the Quarrier family residence. In the hall a large photograph of the founder keeps a stern eye on the activities of the staff. On the desk in the director's office (formerly the Quarrier bedroom) rests a small boot. It was fashioned by Quarrier's own hand when he was a shoe apprentice. It is made from stiff leather, the sole well fortified with hob nails, symbolizing the kind of Scottish durability Quarrier sought to instil in the children. Woe betide the small foot that dared to stray from the path Mr Quarrier's boot set for it.

In Canada, most of the old distributing Homes have been demolished, leaving no trace of the children who came to them. In Peterborough, Ontario, a corner sign 'Barnardo Avenue' recalls the days when Hazel Brae, the Barnardo Home for Girls, stood near it. The story is the same at Niagara-on-the-Lake where, in 1869, Miss Rye took over and renovated the former court-house and jail building for 'Our Western Home'. It too has been torn down, but the street signs 'Rye' and 'Cottage' remind us that thousands of little girls once walked in orderly rows from that corner to St Mark's Anglican Church every Sunday. Marchmont Home, the third building in Belleville to carry the name, is still standing. Fairknowe, the Quarrier Home in Brockville, is one of the few old Homes still in use. It has been converted to an apartment block; its sweeping lawns are confined behind rows of houses and a highway.

The letters published in this volume, The Home Children, were received after an inquiry had been placed in 40 Canadian newspapers indicating my interest in hearing from Canadians or Americans who had come out to this country under the British Child Emigration Movement.

As the replies began to arrive in 1969 and 1970 it became clear that, for many, it was the first time that anyone had asked: 'What was it like to be a "Home Child" in Canada?' How would they express their feelings, relate their experiences—for these children were largely denied the chance for schooling? Despite the expectation that they would attend school on the same basis as the farmer's children, the majority stayed home to herd cows, weed the gardens, or work in the fields, while the farm children went off to school. Often pioneering farmers were unable or saw little necessity to give even their own sons and daughters an education; the Home Child's chances for schooling were even more uncertain.

The letters have been published as they were written with minor editorial changes. In the letters themselves is that quality of durability so frequently found in children and so frequently overlooked—a quality that has been passed on to the second generation.

Two-thirds of the immigrant children were boys, and roughly the same proportion of men have contributed stories. The letters indicate that boys were more inclined to run away from unhappy situations, and their stories contain more variety of experience. The former immigrant girls were expected to be obedient and uncomplaining until their indentures expired and then to marry a 'nice farm boy'.

It was not expected that those people who were overwhelmed by harsh experiences—who may have lived out their lives in prisons or mental institutions—would have replied to the inquiry. Nor have those people who achieved success in federal or provincial governments come forward to tell their stories. Among those successful second-generation Canadians who are proud to be identified with the Home Children are W.A. Cochrane, President and Vice Chancellor of the University of Calgary and son of a Barnardo boy; J.E. Climer, Director of the Saskatoon Gallery and Conservatory Corporation, also the son of a Barnardo boy; and William E.

Taylor, Director of the National Museum of Man, National Museums of Canada, Ottawa, the son of a Stephenson boy.

It is not only the Home Children and their descendants for whom these letters will have meaning. Many Canadians will recognize in the stories someone they knew or heard about long ago: a great aunt perhaps, a grandfather's hired man, or a school friend. There are others still living who had some connection with the distributing Homes, or who crossed the Atlantic on the same ship with a party of children. Perhaps one of the boys who came out on the Doric in August 1929 will recall that a young Oxford student, later to become The Honourable J.W. Pickersgill, a former cabinet minister, was their escort.

The letters show that there was far more abuse and exploitation than Home or Immigration files are likely to reveal. A great deal of faith was placed in written indentures that too many farmers failed to live by as far as schooling and payment of wages agreed upon were concerned. When farmers reneged on wage agreements, the Homes instituted a system of payments directly to the Home. As seen from some of the letters the Homes occasionally lost track of children before their wages could be released to them.

Although the experiences related in these letters are as varied as the contributors, there are some similarities. One is the misunderstanding as to why they were being sent to Canada: 'I thought Canadians had no children' and 'I was told there was a farmer who wanted a boy like me.' Regardless of how old the children were when they emigrated, the strange countryside, the new types of farming ('We saw pails hanging on the trees and wondered what they were'), and above all, the huge engine and its strange whistle when their train left Quebec City to take off to Ontario or Manitoba, were all a source of wonder. Invariably, children were sent from the distributing Home alone, name tags around their necks, to be met by unknown farmers on unknown railway platforms. It was the loneliest moment of their lives. Loneliness looms as the hardest thing to bear in the letters.

To discourage boys from running away from employers, a condition that must have reached epidemic proportions at the height of the emigration of children, 1880 to 1914, medals were given to boys by some Homes. The Barnardo medal indicated these were given for 'Long service and good conduct', but the qualification, in fact, was that the boy had served out his time at his original placement. No case of a girl receiving a medal has been traced. There were girls who did rebel and many had to be removed from undesirable situations, but fewer ran away. Yet the girls were as vulnerable as boys to abuse, although of a different kind. If they were less likely to feel a horsewhip across their backs they were vulnerable to the sexual advances of their employer, his son, or in some cases, a hired man. To add to the girls' dismay, the wives of men who made these advances were often fully aware of their husbands' attentions to the girls. This situation of the girl being left in the house alone with the farmer for a week or two appears in a few of these letters and in some Home visitors' reports. There is a correlation here to recent studies on incest, which also indicate that mothers knowingly contribute to these acts by ignoring what is going on.

Having started from the premise that poverty-stricken children of working-class British families were being given a much greater opportunity in Canada, it is understandable that some people accepted that these children were somehow not like other children—with the same needs for affection, love and understanding. Farmers who seemed insensitive to their young charges often changed their views, as society and knowledge of children's needs changed. Many deeply regretted their previous attitude to the children and tried to make up for it in later years. And lest we think too harshly of the founders who saw child labour on remote Canadian farms as the bright hope for their waifs and strays, let us remember that, for all our sophisticated learning today, there are thousands of children in our own land, and millions throughout the world who suffer from our collective indifference.

How successful was the British Child Emigration Movement? In a time when neither society nor the state accepted responsibility for the care of the poor and when emigration seemed to be the only choice between hunger and plenty, Canada offered hope. The greatest achievement of the child emigration movement, however, was the opportunity it gave to remove children from hopeless situations and to create better lives for their children and grandchildren. The descendants who are now scattered throughout North America are estimated to number over a million. Their contributions to mankind are still to be written, but among them are successful parents, nurses, lawyers, social workers, school principals and business men.

We can all be proud of these citizens who came to Canada as immigrant children, serving out indentures, working in the fields or as house servants until they could strike out on their own, 'free at last'.

Phyllis Harrison
Smithers, British Columbia
October, 1978

Fareham Oct. 2nd 1871

My dear little girl.

We were all very glad to get your nice letter, & it made me very happy to know from your own pen that you are comfortably placed & that your friends are kind to you & you are quite contented with your new home.

I showed your letter to Mr Smith & he praised it very much & shamed Roger because he could not write as good. You must write to Mr Smith Emmy & tell him about your school & the church. He will be so pleased.

I sent your letter to Mrs Greig & she quite cried for joy to hear such good news from you. Mrs Reynolds was very glad too. They have not heard from your brother since you left but no doubt he is well only the ship has been moved on.

How nice it is to know you go to school dear & how very kind your Canadian friends must be to send you. I need not tell you to be a good little girl to deserve such kind treatment for I am sure you will.

I find from a letter received from Miss Rye lately that you are adopted & E. Lewis too & not bound as most of the others are. Tell me when you write again if there are any children where you live & tell me about Ellen Lewis too, as she is not able to write herself you know. Poor little granny! We often talk of her & hope she is happy & good. I suppose she has heard by this time from Adolphus. He sailed 7th Sept for Belleville, Ontario, with six more boys in the care of Miss Macpherson. These are those who went A. Lewis, C. Lee, W. Parsons, G. Goddard, W. Churcher, A. Cooper, & A. Baker.

We have heard from all the girls who can write now, and we know where those are who cannot. A. Cousens is adopted & Mary Churcher & Emma Lee who wrote a very nice letter to her grandmother saying how happy she is. Indeed, you all appear to be very comfortable in your new homes & that is a great comfort to me & your other friends. We often talk of you dear Emmy & the empty long room looks very desolate at night…

• The opening of a letter written to Emily Boys soon after her emigration to Canada. The signature page has not survived but the letter would appear to have been written by a matron of the Fareham Union Workhouse. Published by permission of the High family.

ONE

THE YEARS
1871–1885

Eighty years had not dulled her mind or stiffened her fingers. She could still make chicken pot-pie, doughnuts, and potato soup that tasted better than I can make or anyone else...

My grandmother was one of the first little girls to be brought out to Canada by Miss Maria S. Rye. She sailed in June, 1871 in Miss Rye's fourth party of children. From the Niagara-on-the-Lake Home for orphans, she was taken into the home of Mr and Mrs Daniel Honsberger of Louth township in the Jordan area. Her childhood name was Emily Boys. She was 12 years old.

I can remember my grandmother telling of when the Honsbergers came to get a child. She noticed the couple with the wee baby and she wished she could go to where the baby lived. Then the man came over and asked her if she would like to live with them.

Grandmother often wondered in her later years why Grandpa and Grandma Honsberger, as she came to know them, chose to take her into their family. I believe that they had two other small children as well as the baby. They may have needed an older child to watch over the little ones while the mother was in the barn milking, or in the garden, or doing another of the many time-consuming tasks of pioneer families. The Honsberger family was of German origin and of the Mennonite faith. Their grandparents had moved from Pennsylvania to Louth township about 1805. They did not believe it proper to fight their fellow men and refused to take up arms during a civil uprising in the States. They strictly followed the Christian ideals of helping one another to live useful and peaceful lives. These were the values that my grandmother learned as a young

11

woman in her Ontario home and she lived by these beliefs until her death in 1956 at the age of 97.

In 1877 grandmother was married to Jonas High, the son of another family of Pennsylvanian origin. They continued to live at Jordan Station and four children were born to them. One daughter, Stella, still survives, living in her own home in Toronto at the age of 83. She has a remarkable vitality—one of her mother's characteristics. Jonas died in 1894 of pneumonia when my father, Roy High, was 18 months old. About four years later grandmother married Henry High of South Cayuga, a cousin of her first husband.

I have fond memories of my grandmother. She lived in my father's home in her 80s—but 80 years had not dulled her mind or stiffened her fingers. She could still make chicken pot-pie, doughnuts and potato soup that tasted better than I can make even though I follow her recipes faithfully.

Grandmother was a good home seamstress and an expert butcher's helper. She would go to other homes and help with the butchering even in her later days. During her middle years she would go out in the community and act as a mid-wife when a new baby arrived. After her second husband died she was companion and housekeeper for an elderly couple until she was nearly 80. Her favourite pastime was to knit lace of fine cotton on needles made from hat pins. It was her joy to make these lace doilies and give them to her family and her many friends. The whole community knew her as Grandma High.

Grandmother never lost pride in her English ancestry, but I am certain that the circumstances that caused her to be in an orphanage always remained a mystery to her. On her birth certificate her parents' names are given as Sarah Burgess Boys and Edward Boys and her place of birth was Portland Street, Fareham. Her father was a carpenter and she had a brother who was also a carpenter. Today she has 94 living descendants.

Grandmother always thought she was an orphan and this has now been confirmed by the records. Whatever the circumstances, she was one little girl who came to Canada and found a new home through the kindness and generosity of Miss Rye.

Emily Boys
as told by her granddaughter
Mrs John Moyer
Fenwick, Ontario

The family mother was with believed in taking more than their 'pound of flesh'.

Our mother did not want us to know that she was a little immigrant girl. As we grew older we assumed that this was because she thought that we, her family, and the members of the community might look down on her. We do not have much information on her childhood and in the bit she told us there was very little happiness.

However, she did tell us that she came to Canada at six years of age to a farm near Port Hope, Ontario. As her birthdate was in May 1872 I assume that she arrived in 1878. I believe that her little sister arrived at the same time but was not taken by the same family.

The family that mother was with believed in taking more than their 'pound of flesh', for when she reached the age that she was to be paid for her household labours they defaulted. Her wages were set at $6.00 a year.

Another vivid item she told us about was her first menstruation. Of course she had not been told anything, and when it occurred she was frantic with fear. In her panic she attempted to clean up in the watering trough and as a consequence she was ill.

Mother's maiden name was Emma Kennett, and when she was 18 she married my father, Joseph Magahay, who was a young widower with a small daughter, Mae. The daughter lived with her mother's sister. For many years my parents lived at Mount Horeb. Their home was situated at the top of a hill approached by road from three directions.

Years ago when children walked everywhere, especially to school and church, a great many of them had to pass our door. A goodly number of these children were also from 'The Home' and were not always dressed the best or the warmest for the Ontario winters. Not once, but many times I have seen mother watch for these children and take them out her hand-knit mitts, and put them on cold little hands, or a new little cotton dress or shirt in summer. Sundays in the summer usually meant watching for children returning from Sunday school and treating them to slices of watermelon or some home-baked treat.

This was the kind of woman our mother grew into and she was known throughout the community for her hospitality, and all the kind acts she always performed so quietly and unassumingly. We were a happy family—lots of work, lots of love, lots of discipline—and certainly we received a good example in morals from our parents.

Mother died December 2, 1934, and is buried in the cemetery at Mount Horeb Church. Our biggest regret is that she did not live to know very many of her grandchildren whom I know she would have loved, and they, her.

Emma Magahay, née Kennett
as told by *her daughter*
Mrs Marguerite Kemp
Peterborough, Ontario

I realize how much more I would love to know about his life. But he would never talk about it.

My dad said that his mother arrived at the dockside to see him off and he could remember her sobbing as she watched the ship sail away. He never saw her again.

My dad's name was William Jeffrey Baldwin. He was born in Surrey, England, May 27, 1876. His own father, Robert Gordon Baldwin, was killed in the African Zulu War when dad was about five years of age. After this his mother (born Anne Jeffrey, a governess) went to France taking her boy with her. Eventually she came back and put dad in the care of elderly aunts but it is presumed they were unable to cope with the small boy; his mother, as a governess, was not permitted to have him with her. He was put in Mr Fegan's Home—which one I do not know. While there the headmaster asked the boys if any of them would like to go to Canada and my dad said 'Yes'.

I expect he arrived in the Toronto Home and from there went to a farm where he remembered having to get up at daybreak and feed, water, curry, and harness horses before ploughing the fields. He was nine years of age and how long he worked there, he never said. But from there he went to work for a doctor, driving the horse and carriage while the rounds were made and avidly learning all he could.

What he earned he must have saved and when 18 or 19 years of age he came to British Columbia, settling on the lower mainland in the District of Surrey where he eventually bought property. He went to school in Cloverdale to get his primary education, and then studied at home to become a stationary engineer. Dad died in 1945 and since he has gone I realize how much more about his life I would love to know. But he would never talk about it to any extent and being so young when he came to Canada he could not remember many details of his early years. He kept his letters, Bible, and pictures of his mother in the church at Hazelmere, which he helped build, and where he thought they would be safe. The church burned down and he lost all of this including his mother's address. He never knew what happened to her.

William Jeffrey Baldwin
as told by his daughter
Miss Geraldine Baldwin
Surrey, British Columbia

I cannot remember the sale of the Barnardo farm and buildings at Russell, Manitoba... but I can remember dad speaking about it.

My father, George Fisher, was a boy of 16 when he came to Canada in 1883. He went first to Niagara, Ontario, and after a brief stay, he came out to Russell, Manitoba, and worked on the Barnardo farm for some years. When a new group of boys came in he helped them with the work. The young boys had no knowledge of farming and my father himself was never on a farm until he came here. Mr E.A. Struthers was the foreman at the Barnardo farm when my father arrived.

Around 1888 dad bought a quarter section of land (section 19, township 20, range 28) from the Home. He paid $5.00 an acre for it. Then he bought a team of horses and built a small frame cottage. This cottage is still standing, but it has not been lived in since around 1964.

Around the turn of the century my dad sold one acre of land to the government to build a school on it. Craigie school operated for many years, but it has now been closed and they sold the land back to my sister who owns the original property.

My father and mother were married in 1897 in the church at the Barnardo farm. Mother passed away in December 1910 and dad raised our family of four. Now there is just the two of us left, my sister and me.

I cannot remember the sale of the Barnardo farm and buildings. I was too young, but I remember dad speaking about it. Our farm was two miles away from the main buildings. Our first post office was in the Home building and Mr Struthers was the post master.

My father died on the 8 September 1945. He always spoke well of the treatment he received while working for Dr Barnardo.

George Fisher
as told by his daughter
Mrs Mary Olafson
Lundar, Manitoba

At seven years, she was placed in a home where the mother was blind. She worked very hard.

My grandmother came out to Ontario when I was about four years old. I had to sleep with her and all I can remember about her was that she had bright red corsets. I never cared for her because of her sending her two little girls to far-off Canada.

My mother, Minnie Esther Ashmore, was seven years old in 1878 when she was sent over. She was not supposed to be parted from her sister who was two years older. But parted they were—although they still attended the same school. My mother was placed in a home where the mother was blind. There were five young men in the home—three of them died of tuberculosis. My mother worked very hard.

In 1893 she married my father and they raised six children. They had happy days and sad days. My father passed away in 1955, and that same year my mother was shot in the neck by a person who was deranged. She lost her mind over it. This tragic happening will never be forgotten by her family.

There were quite a number of boys who came to this district from the Barnardo homes from 1910 to 1925. Some of them have moved on to parts unknown.

Minnie Esther Ashmore
as told by her daughter
Mrs Minnie Gentleman
Melbourne, Ontario

The father hoped to emigrate later and join his sons, but this never happened.

Three brothers, ages five and seven and nine, came to Canada from Birmingham in May 1877. My father, Thomas Loach, was the youngest one. Their mother had died the previous year leaving the father with five children to raise. In October 1876 he placed the three boys in an orphanage and gave permission for them to be sent to Canada but not for their adoption.

I don't know at what port the ship docked or where the children were first sent. But the Loach boys were raised by three separate farm families living in the same community. I know that the people who took dad were named Snell and must have lived in Mulmur Township, Ontario. He used to talk about his childhood there.

I learned from records in England that the years of birth of the Loach boys were wrong. Their father or the Home must have registered them all as two years older than they were. Possibly this was because a five-year-old would be too young to send overseas. The father hoped to emigrate later and join his sons, but this never happened.

The children of the three brothers correspond and visit one another regularly. Joseph's four in Los Angeles; William's in Kansas City and San Francisco; and Thomas's in Ontario. In each case a grandson is carrying on the family name—Joe, Bill and Tom.

Thomas Loach
as told by his daughter
Miss Laura Loach
Kirkland Lake, Ontario

She spoke of sitting at her mother's feet in this factory, playing with spools.

'You shouldn't feel like that. At least you don't know what it is to feel no one cares if you live or die and wants you only if you can work hard.' That is what my mother, Agnes Short, used to say to us when we complained of something. She was a sensitive and loving person.

I recall her speaking of being brought over by the Barnardo Home around 1880 when she was five years old. Mother was a Scot and her home was in Glasgow. When she first came to Canada she was put with an old couple whose family was grown up and away. This was in the Ottawa or Burritts Rapids area.

She was fond of these folks and I feel they were good to her. Later, when the man whom she called Grampa died, she was sent here and there to relatives where there was sickness or help needed. I remember her speaking of doing large family washes at one of these places at the age of 10 years. She milked cows at a younger age than that. She was a tiny person, got little education, and worked very hard.

When she was in her teens she found out that her father had been sick a long time. Her mother worked in a factory, and my mother spoke of sitting at her mother's feet in this factory playing with spools. But the time came when her mother could not manage alone and she put my mother in a Home. From there she was sent to Canada.

Agnes McFadden, née Short
as told by her daughter
Mrs Mary Baillie
Terrace Bay, Ontario

THE YEARS
1888 – 1899

There was no tender kiss on the cheek no kindly handshake...in meeting this small Scottish boy.

In 1894 when Mr Quarrier came to Cottage No. 26 at Bridge-of-Weir to make up his list to go to Canada, he told me what a wonderful place it was, and that I had a sister living not far from Belleville, Ontario. You can imagine the thrill, the excitement, the enthusiasm of such a prospect: to cross the mighty ocean, travel miles by train to meet an unknown sister, see new people and new lands. It was all too much for a 10-year-old boy to contain so I said 'Yes'.

We were 18 days reaching Halifax, and sat and slept on the slats in colonist cars to Brockville. A big boy looked after a small one. The menu was very plain. It took me three days to reach the farm in Monteagle Township, 175 miles from Brockville. I travelled by train to Ormsby the first day, then 16 miles to Bancroft on the old stage coach that carried the mail, and by wagon to the farm on the third day.

It was nice meeting my sister, Sara, but still I had the feeling of meeting a stranger. James and Elizabeth Price, who were to be my foster parents for the next 12 years, were 40 years old at the time. There was no tender kiss on the cheek, no kindly handshake, no enthusiasm shown in meeting this small Scottish boy. It was just a matter-of-fact meeting. After the excitement had worn off I tried to adapt myself to the new surroundings. It wasn't just as easy as I had thought. Facing the realities of life was no easy problem for a young boy. No doubt being with my sister helped me greatly to adjust. After I had proven my worth around the farm, life straightened out. I became contented and satisfied with my lot.

North Hastings is a rolling, rocky, beautiful country, but at the time of my arrival it was primitive indeed. It was all hard work. There were no machines until about 1905. The grain was cut with the grain cradle, the hay with the scythe, the hand rake was in general use, and also the hoe. Threshing was done with a circular horse-powered thresher. Log buildings and fences were on every farm, and very often the house was built of logs too. The people were a hardy lot, hard-working and economical by nature and circumstance. A hired man got 50 cents a day and board. It was here that I learned the importance of work and saving.

I had a very good home, good food mostly produced on the farm, and modest but good clothes. The wool was taken from the sheep's back, very often carded by hand and spun into yarn on the old spinning wheel. Women would spend their winter evenings knitting socks and mitts. Some had the loom and wove the yarn into cloth and flannel for warm winter wear. There were a number of cheese factories in the area, but all our cream from 10 cows was churned into butter in the old dash churn.

I attended church, sang in the choir and many times walked the four miles there and back. As a youth I was aghast at those old tight farmers putting 25 cents on the collection plate and taking off 10 or 15 cents in change. The minister lived on a mere pittance, and school teachers got $250 yearly.

The social life was handmade. There were picnics, dances, house parties, ball games, sleigh riding, and snowshoeing; and the church concert held annually at Christmas was greatly anticipated. Recitations, dialogues, and singing were carried on with gusto. I loved to recite and generally had two or three recitations. The Family Herald was about the only news medium. Communication with the outside world was limited until the railroad came in 1901.

I walked two miles to school and here is my most serious complaint. The Quarrier Homes had a written agreement with my foster parents that they would send me to school until I would pass my entrance, but I was taken out when I finished the old second reader. They didn't put much value on education. Now it is so important. How did I get along without any? It must have been self-initiative. In my early manhood I vowed that if I ever had children they would be educated, and they were. And further, if I could help others I would, and I did. Working with the reeve of Bancroft and the public school inspector, we established the North Hastings High School in the village. I was the first chairman of the board and my name, as such, is on a plaque at the front entrance. There are nearly 1,000 students attending today.

19

Today I pay tribute to the memory of William Quarrier and my foster parents. They gave me shelter, food, and care when I was adrift in poverty and despair. (He is the God that giveth the desolate a home to dwell in, Psalm 68-6.) I thank Him for the day when I first stepped on Canadian soil. No doubt it was the unseen hand that directed me in the way I should go. Today we live in serene happiness, surrounded by a wonderful family, with many friends throughout Hastings County and a comfortable home with plenty to keep us to the end and more.

J.L. Churcher
Bancroft, Ontario

A bunch of horses got on the track and just kept running ahead of the train. The engine struck one and wound it around the wheels...

When I arrived in Toronto from England in the fall of 1896 I was sent to live with some nice Jewish people—a mother and two sons by the name of Philips. Harry and Jimmy wore their hair long but they were very fine people. Where they lived it was called the Commons. It was a mile or so back in a field in Toronto. I was there for a few months. It was just a temporary home.

From there I was sent to St Catharines where I was met by a farmer who took me home. There were several Home boys around St Catharines and most had good homes but I found it different. I am sorry to say that I was abused. All this man cared about was the $5.00 a month that he was paid by the Home and all the work he could get out of me.

The land was half bush. The old man would get the horse and go out and cut down a big tree and drag it to the house. I would have to cut it up for the stoves. I cut wood before I went to school in the morning and after I came home at night. I got as far as junior fourth in school.

Then I got a job with some people doing chores, such as carrying water for the house at 40 cents a day, 10 hours a day. It took all the money I earned to pay my board. Then I got a job at Brown Bros Nursery. I was paid 75 cents a day, worked 10 hours and paid $2.50 a week for board. I saved a few dollars.

I had heard a lot about the West and thought I would try it, so I left Toronto by train for Alberta. It took four days and nights at that time. There were no fences; the railroad just ran across the prairies. Hundreds of wild horses and cattle roamed all over. A bunch of horses got on the track and kept running just ahead of the train. The engine struck one and wound it around the wheels and the train stopped.

When I got to Alberta I found things very expensive. You needed a lot of money and I had very little. I got work among the settlers at about $10 a month. At night I could see and hear the wolves trying to get at the cattle. The church was a log schoolhouse and we went on Sundays in the lumber wagon. There were a few Indians about but they would not harm anyone.

I headed east early in the fall and stopped off in a place called Alexander in Manitoba. I was about 16 years old. I got a job bucking straw with a man who had his own threshing outfit with six men. After the threshing I came back to Ontario and worked for two or three years in Welland in a nursery. As time went on I saved $550 and bought 10 acres of bare land. That used up my money so I went to the mill, got some lumber and built myself a shack. I worked in nurseries in the day and on the land at nights. I borrowed $150 from the bank to buy my first horse and $600 towards building my house.

I have had plenty of experiences through my life but I've fought my way through. I now have a small farm and a nice home here.

Robert Bishop
Fenwick, Ontario

I married her because the old gentleman told me I should. He said she was a good cook.

About 35 years ago we had a cottage on Happy Lake near Bissett, Manitoba, and there I met English John, a well-known trapper, who had come to Canada as a Barnardo boy at the age of 10. Over the years we became friends and he told me his life story. When he could no longer live alone, we made arrangements for his care in the St Norbert Lodge where his room looks out on the Red River.

English John—John Henry Thomas—was born in Tuckingmill, Cornwall, England, on October 19, 1887. His father, a tin miner, was killed by a train when John was a small child. His mother remarried and began to raise a second family. John and his stepfather were never on good terms. When the stepfather drank he abused John and at the age of seven or eight he began running away from home. After several attempts to escape, John was given the choice of being returned to his home by the police or being sent to the Barnardo Home in London. He welcomed the chance to go to Stepney and spent two years there.

At the age of 10 he was included in a group of children who sailed for Canada. John does not remember the year, but it would be 1897 or 1898. He was indentured to a farmer near Stonewall, 15 miles north of Winnipeg. There he spent the winter, carrying wood and water, helping to feed the cattle and doing dishes and other household chores. He attended the country school for a short time.

John soon tired of farm life and in the early spring he decided to run away. He tramped the country roads back to Winnipeg and found his first job washing dishes for his room and board in a restaurant on Main Street.

Over the next two years he wandered south of the border to the out-skirts of Minneapolis, Minnesota. He followed the railroad tracks or the country roads—stopping at farms, doing chores, and sleeping in barns or haystacks along the way. Many of the farmers were willing to have him stay with them indefinitely, for he was a cheerful and willing worker. But he preferred to wander.

In his travels he came upon a discarded boat on the bank of the Red River. He paddled it along with the current towards the Manitoba border. At the bend of the river in North Dakota, he met a man travelling in the same direction. His name was Boudrais, a carpenter by trade, just returned from an unsuccessful venture in the Yukon Gold Rush. Boudrais had a sound and sturdy row boat, so he suggested to John that he discard the old craft and join him. Together they travelled down the Red River to Winnipeg. At the junction of the Red and Assiniboine Rivers they camped and fished for goldeye. John peddled the fish to homes and restaurants nearby, in exchange for bread and tea.

They continued their journey down the Red, past Lockport, Selkirk, and other small settlements to the mouth of the river and into Lake Winnipeg. Following the east shore, they rowed north to the settlement of Manigotagan—also known as Bad Throat. This journey took several weeks, for they were often storm-bound on Lake Winnipeg.

Boudrais found employment at the sawmill at Manigotagan. John, still a boy, found only chores to do—carrying water and wood. Eventually Boudrais travelled on his way and a Saulteaux Indian family by the name of Bunn 'adopted' John. The family consisted of one son, Roderick, and three adopted daughters. John Bunn, the father, was of medium height, stocky and powerful. With a head strap, he could carry a large bear or a caribou on his back. He was an experienced and successful trapper, built his own birch-bark canoes and his log cabins. He taught John about the roots, berries, and herbs to collect and use in times of illness, showed him the wild onion for flavouring food, and the wild cranberry to make smudges for mosquitoes and black-flies. This practical knowledge enabled John to survive and enjoy life in the wilderness when he was left to his own resources.

Mrs Bunn, a kindly woman, short and stout, took a motherly interest in John. He held her in high regard and kept in touch with her until her death. The Bunns understood some English and this enabled John to learn their native language more easily. After a year he was fluent in Saulteaux and Cree—the only languages he ever heard on the traplines. He scarcely heard English spoken for over 30 years. When he went into a settlement, he found English strange to his ears and felt shy about using it.

In the autumn before the lake and river would freeze over, the Bunn family would leave Manigotagan for the trapline on Clearwater Lake. The canoes would be loaded with traps and food supplies, sled dogs, harnesses and toboggans. They would journey up the Manigotagan River, camping and portaging.

At Clearwater Lake John Bunn had a small log cabin and this is where English John spent his first winter in the bush. He carried firewood, cut a water-hole in the ice for a water supply and snared rabbits and grouse for the soup pot. Most of the meat was provided by Mr Bunn who shot deer, moose and caribou. They supplemented their diet of meat and fish with wild rice, bannock and tea.

Every morning John Bunn would leave by dog-team to inspect his traps. Beaver were not plentiful, but there was an abundance of mink, otter, fisher, wolverine, marten, fox, weasel and lynx. The carcasses, when released from the traps, were usually frozen solid and had to be thawed out in the cabin. Members of the family helped to skin them, put them on stretchers, and hang them from the ceiling to dry.

In the early spring when the trapping season ended, the family returned to Manigotagan. The furs were traded at the Hudson's Bay Company post at Fort Alexander, about 40 miles south on the Winnipeg River.

During the summer John and Mrs Bunn set out fish nets in the lake and river. Fish were plentiful in numbers and variety: pike, pickerel, whitefish, goldeye, and sturgeon. John sold the sturgeon to Arthur Quesnell who ran a 'stopping place' in Manigotagan. On one occasion a sudden squall came up on the lake when John and Mrs Bunn were some distance from shore. Neither could swim. Mrs Bunn became frightened in the small tippy canoe. They had just finished pulling in a net and had a metal tub full of fish in the boat. John emptied them overboard and held up the tub for a sail. This brought them safely to shore in a few minutes.

John lived and travelled with the Bunn Family for many years. He and John Bunn became partners, sharing the trapline and its profits. When Mr Bunn died, John inherited his trapline. (The only son, Roderick, had died in a flu epidemic.) When John was in his 20s, he married Sara James, a 50-year-old Indian woman. They had no children.

'She was too old' said English John. 'I married her because the old gentleman (as he always called Mr Bunn) told me I should. He said she was a good cook.'

John acquired a homestead—which he called Quon de Gog—on Lake Winnipeg, six miles north of Fort Alexander. Here, he and Sara lived for several years. When John was away on the trapline, Sara would trap on the homestead and shoot moose and deer. She skinned and hung these herself. At one time John was away in the Hudson Bay area for five years.

'Well, the old lady was still waiting for me' John said, telling of his return to his homestead. He also trapped at Norway House and around York Factory.

After Sara died, John built a log cabin at Happy Lake which was on his trapline. He spent his winters there and in the summer he would fish commercially on Lake Winnipeg, or stay in Bissett. During the years of World War II, my husband and I and others from Bissett built a cottage at Happy Lake, and there we got to know English John. He enjoyed having neighbours and began to spend his summers there. He planted a vegetable garden which he shared with us, and he built an icehouse to supply us with ice which he cut in the early spring.

In 1952, a reporter attending the trappers' banquet in Bissett wrote an article about English John. A children's newspaper carried the story, and in a town in Cornwall, England, a man read the story to his mother. She exclaimed 'That is my brother'. After a number of letters to the Royal Canadian Mounted Police, they established the fact that John was, indeed, her brother. She wrote to him and I read him the letters and helped him to answer them.

In February 1969 John became seriously ill, and was rushed to a hospital in Winnipeg. After surgery and several months in the hospital, English John realized that his trapping days had come to an end. He moved to a senior citizens' home in St Norbert, Manitoba, in September, 1969. There, at 86 years of age he is still active, caring for his small vegetable garden beside the lodge and ringing the bell at mealtimes.

John Henry Thomas
recorded by one of his friends, Florence Caswell, Winnipeg, Manitoba, 1974

Henry brought her a bag of cookies and said 'goodbye'.

Elizabeth Owen, my mother, always longed to know who her mother and father were. She had a brother, Henry, six years older. She remembers that when he was 14 years old he was taken from the orphanage where they were together in England. The man who took him was going to teach him to be a baker. When my mother got on the boat to leave for Canada, Henry brought her a bag of cookies and said 'Goodbye'.

My mother was born in England on March 9, 1882, and was around eight years of age when she came to Canada. From the Home at Niagara-on-the-Lake she was adopted by a Mr and Mrs Wood from Hagersville, Ontario. They changed her name to Lillie Beatrice Wood. She had a wonderful home, was sent to school and church. At the age of 21 she was married to a good man. I am one of five daughters born to them.

Mother died in March 1967. I would like to find some of her relatives in England.

Lillie Beatrice Wood, née Elizabeth Owen
as told by her daughter
whose name is withheld by request.

She was always very careful not to tell us anything concerning her childhood.

My mother and a younger brother were left orphans at the ages of eleven and seven. They were taken to the Barnardo Home at Stepney and two years later, in about 1897, they were sent out to Toronto. My mother was taken into the home of a childless couple at Schomberg, Ontario. Her adopted parents gave her everything with much love added.

Her brother, George, on the other hand, at the age of 10 was taken to a farm about 50 miles north of Toronto. Here he was made to work early and late with only the clothes given to him at the Home. After a summer of hard work he was turned out at four o'clock one afternoon on a cold snowy day. He had holes worn completely through his shoes and no warm clothing. This sad state of affairs never left his mind. At the age of 84, he sat at my kitchen table and told me the story with tears flowing freely.

I also had an aunt by marriage whom, I feel sure, came to Canada as an immigrant child. She has just recently passed away at the age of 89. She was always careful not to tell us anything concerning her childhood, except that a sister came with her. The sister somehow ended up in Regina. After her death, a stranger whom she had confided in, told her story to us.

Emily King as told by her daughter
Mrs. Emily Johnson
Weston, Ontario

After it was over he came and shook hands with me and asked if I would forgive him, which I did...

Our father was a butcher, I remember. Then he took work at a pottery firm and while he was there he took very sick and died. He would be about 55 or 56 and I believe the year was 1888. There were six brothers and one sister in our family. My brother Charles and I would have been six and eight years of age. At that time Jack the Ripper was on the go. Mother told us not to wander too far from home or he would get us.

Mother's youngest sister persuaded mother to put Charles and me into Dr Barnardo's Home at Stepney Causeway in London. They took us there and it was all right until they kissed us goodbye. Then they left and we both stood there and cried until we could cry no more. The man took us inside, bathed us and gave us Home clothes to put on.

When it came time to be transferred, my brother Charles was sent to Toronto. As for me, I went to the Isle of Jersey where they sent sickly boys to get the sea breezes and bring them around to good health. I helped to wash dishes and wipe them and some afternoons they took us down to Bully Bay and taught us to swim and to catch crabs. As time went on I learned to play the B flat horn and went into the boys' band. We would play carols and sing and most folk enjoyed our music. One time the band was invited to the Isle of Guernsey where we stayed in people's homes. Another boy and me were sent to a lovely home. When we went to bed we sunk into real feathers.

I must have been at the Island for five years. I asked one of the men if there was any chance of going to Canada to be near my brother. He said that if I improved I might go with the next lot of boys, and I did. The trip across the ocean was rough and most of us were seasick. We docked in Halifax, then went by train to Toronto and out to the Home on Farley Avenue. I had to stay there some time. I received some letters from mother and the Boy's Own Paper and books called Chums.

Well, it came to the time that I was placed with a gardener at London, Ontario. My clothes and trunk were fixed up and off I went. It was arranged by paper that I would work there five years for the sum of $75. This gardener was the third heaviest man in London. I learned most of my gardening from him. He had two gardens—one of 15 acres at their home, and another of 15 acres out at Glendale—a drive of five miles. The garden in Glendale consisted of strawberries—about two acres of them—and two or three acres of raspberries and a small orchard of apple trees. The balance was in meadow. He also raised Light Brahma and Buff Orpington hens which he exhibited. I would be given the job of grooming them by plucking one feather at a time. The hen house was always kept warm. At the fall fair his hens took first, second, and third prizes. His vegetables took prizes too.

A man from the Home came around to see if I was all right and I said I was treated nice. I put in my five years and hired out for another year. That sixth year I took a sick spell and they called the doctor. He said it was rheumatic fever and ordered me to the hospital. My mistress asked me if I would let her take care of me and I said 'Yes, if I'm not any trouble.' I was given every chance to get over this sickness.

My brother would often come to see me on his bicycle. My boss thought he was coming too often and putting bad thoughts in my head which he never did. Shortly after my illness he came to see me and my boss swore at him and I didn't think much of that. I asked for my money and my trunk and left. I was standing at the tracks on Richmond Street when a man I had spoken to before came along and asked me what was wrong. So I told him. He took me to his place and I had breakfast and supper there.

By this time my brother and I had some money so we thought we would go back to our mother. She often mentioned this in her letters and we did not need coaxing. So we went to the Canadian Pacific Railway station and bought tickets from London, Ontario, to Old London, England. It was not long before we were at our mother's door. We were kissed and hugged and taken inside where we all had a drink together for good luck. I never touch liquor so I had a bottle of ginger beer.

I tried to get work in London at Wm Whitleys, the department store. The foreman asked me if I had a recommendation. I said 'No'. I wrote for a reference to my boss in Ontario and v' he wrote back he asked me to come and work for him. I replied 'Not without my brother.' So in the end, he sent a cheque to pay for both of us and I promised to stay with him for five years.

We sailed on the Tunisian to Montreal, and then we took the train to London, Ontario, where my boss met us and drove us back to the farm for supper. My brother had a job with a neighbour and I started back at planting strawberries, stacking grain, and loading hay. As time went on my boss started up a bus route from Fernhill to London. He took folks for 35 cents one way or 55 cents return, and he took in farm produce and sold it and would bring back barrels of soda biscuits. He would buy them for $1.00 and sell them for $1.25.

After my five years were up I bought 15 acres of land from my boss's dad. I paid $300 down and $100 a year and taxes, which I thought was easy payment. I could pick 200 quarts of strawberries a day and sell them at five cents to seven cents a quart. Then I bought a heifer in calf for $65 and a couple of young pigs.

During this time I would often go out to see my brother. The people he lived with were on the outskirts of Strathroy—a Mr and Mrs Hardy. Sometimes my boss would let me take the horse and cart and sometimes I would walk the 11 miles and arrive there Sunday morning while these folks were having breakfast. Several times my brother said 'You don't come to see me, but Myrtle.' I really came to see them both, for I thought she was the girl for me. We spent what little time I had, together. Her dad was an engineer in the powerhouse in Strathroy, but he wanted to leave, so when he had a chance he went west to Brandon, Manitoba, with his family. Myrtle and I were a long way from one another. We used to write, although her mother tried to keep us apart. Myrtle got a chance for me to work in Brandon at $35 a month which seemed all right with me.

In the meantime I was still working for my boss in Fernhill. One Sunday morning we had words and he jumped up and tried to choke me, and his fingers sank into my neck until it bled. He was cross; whether he was tired or wasn't doing well on the bus route, I don't know. He came at me again and I ran out and spent the night with my chum. In the morning they drove me into Ailsa Craig and I lodged a complaint. The case came up in court and he pleaded guilty. After it was over he came and shook hands with me and asked if I would forgive him, which I did. He was so good to me after that and helped me put in my crop. I had 15 acres and a patch of strawberries and everything was in good shape, so I hit out for Brandon. My brother ran the garden and my boss looked after the crop and sent me the money from it.

So I worked for this farmer at $35 a month and stayed with him until the wedding. Our wedding day was 28 October—her mother's birthday. Her mother said it was an awful present. We had a lovely wedding, even to the Baptist minister who proclaimed us married. The next day I bought train tickets for the East. We arrived back in Ontario and all our neighbours were there to greet us, and my wife felt at home.

Percy Ashby
Victoria, B.C.
Published by permission of his daughter
Mrs Helen Roe, Brandon, Manitoba.

I can still remember my first meal with them... canned salmon and peas, warmed together in a pan... delicious.

'There are no taps in the country and no roads, only trails' I wrote to my mother from Canada in 1899. 'Everyone has to bake their own bread, make their own butter and jam and chop their own wood!' My mother kept my letters and gave them back to me. I still have two of them to remind me of those years.

I sailed to Quebec City aboard the Arawa. Some of the boys went to the Barnardo Home in Toronto, and others—of which I was one—went on to Winnipeg for a few days. While there I was introduced to cutting wood by means of a bucksaw and saw-horse.

From Winnipeg I travelled to Qu'Appelle by train and then on to Fort Qu'Appelle by stage coach. I saw water drawn from a well, and drinking pails for the first time. The farmer who took me was John White. He lived 16 miles north of the Fort, was married, and had a son David, and a hired man. I was taught to help in the house—drying dishes—and to feed cattle and horses, buck wood and later, milk cows. I was once called upon to milk all the cows, about 12 of them, when David was away for a day or two. The next year I learned to drive a team of horses and to harrow—walking behind the harrows, as it was usually done in those days. I also learned to ride a horse and to bring the cattle back home at night. I cannot remember the food, but it was no doubt good and I grew well on it. We attended church every Sunday. A Church of England service was held at Charles Neil's farm one Sunday and a Presbyterian service was held on the next Sunday in another home. I remember winning 10 cents in a race at a picnic—my first Canadian money. Nothing was said about school. There was no compulsory education in those days and it was five years before I was able to attend school in Canada. I had been in standard three in England and could read and write quite well.

Life went on like that for three or so years. Once I was unhappy and ran away and Sergeant Fyffe of the Royal North West Mounted Police took me back. He gave me good advice, but I ran away again and spent some time with Mr and Mrs John Redpath, an elderly Scottish couple. Their farm was a few miles west of the Whites and across Jumping Deer Creek.

From there I went to Sam Redpath's—one of the sons. He was a struggling rancher, married and with small children. There I learned what real work was like. I was expected to do a man's work pitching hay onto a stack while Sam was on the stack building it up.

I spent one winter with Mr and Mrs J.C. Wood who farmed on the north side of the Qu'Appelle Valley above where the sanitorium was later built. I helped to haul grain from the farm to Qu'Appelle via the Fort, three times weekly in fair weather. We would bag and tie the grain and load it the day before on sleighs. The next morning we would set out with two loads and drive to the elevators, unload them, have lunch and start back, arriving about nine o'clock at night.

There was considerable visiting with other farmers and drivers on the road. Several sleighs would be in line. The horses would pull the loads and the drivers would tie the lines together for a blather—as the Scots say. On the return journey the speed of the horses would vary and the sleighs would become more scattered. It was a cold winter and I froze my nose, ears and chin, and sores developed. I had a disagreement with Mr Wood— newly married—and spent a month or two with a German bachelor who was also a rancher. He was supposed to pay me $1.00 a day, but paid me off with only one silver dollar.

In the spring of 1903 I joined myself to Mr and Mrs Thomas H. Barnes of the Fort. They had a son Harry, younger than me by a couple of years, and three girls who were all younger than Harry. They all attended school at the Fort. Here, I found a friendship that lasted after the death of the two parents. I must have been hungry when I came, for I can still remember my first meal with them—canned salmon and peas, warmed together in a pan. I thought it was delicious.

There was no school for me. We had work to do. Mr Barnes kept a stable and horses across the street from his home, and his work was meeting incoming settlers and taking them to see homestead lands that were still open north of the valley. He used to come back, paid off with British sovereigns.

Harry and I used to go south of the valley and get hay and firewood to use at home. We also took loads to the homestead that Mr Barnes had on the Loon Creek plain. On one occasion we were taking a load of poles to the homestead with a team of oxen. The oxen plodded along. Whenever they felt like a drink they would head for the nearest slough and drink, no matter what Harry and I wished. It was a slow trip. Dark came before we reached the homestead and we had to camp under the load, light a fire to keep off the mosquitoes, and finish our journey to the homestead the next morning.

That fall I shot my first wild crane by stalking it on horseback. These birds had long legs and could see over the stooks. Their meat was very tasty.

The winter of 1903-04 was one of the worst in years. Snow was six feet deep on the level and snowbanks in the Fort were high enough to step over the telegraph line which ran down the main street; steps were cut to get down to the stores. I learned to skate that winter, on skates which fastened to my ordinary boots with side clamps and a lever. It was the custom to build the rink on the river which skirted the north edge of town, using poles and straw for the sides and roof. In the spring the poles were removed and the debris floated down the river. It was a very cheap skating rink. That spring the river overflowed its banks and flooded the flats and fish were everywhere. The bridge was covered and lights hung at each end to guide travellers. There has not been such a flood since.

The spring of 1904 brought a big change to the Barnes family and to me. The Pheasant Hills Branch of the Canadian Pacific Railway was being built from Kirkella to Saskatoon, and small villages and hamlets were springing up all along the line about seven or eight miles apart.

The line had reached Balcarres some 16 miles north-east of the Fort the fall before. Mr Barnes accepted the position of managing a new lumber yard in Balcarres and I, of course, went along. The job of moving nearly cost me my life. I was driving the team and wagon with a grain box back to the Fort for another load when I came to a ford over the Qu'Appelle River north-east of town. It was spring and the snow had gone, but the river ice was still in position. I walked out onto the ice to test it and it gave way and I fell in up to my neck. I was able to scramble out, soaking wet, and drove the team to town around by the bridge, wet and shivering.

When we got to Balcarres, I was at last able to attend school. I took part in sports, helped in the general store and post office, and in the tinshop where I learned to make stovepipes. I have many pleasant memories of my life in Balcarres.

After four years I accepted a job at Cupar with John Hubbs, a real estate and insurance agent. Mr Hubbs had a large farmhouse on the outskirts of Cupar. I had a room in his attic and worked in the office—a small frame building of two rooms next door to the Union Bank. I was paid $25 a month and my board. Mr Hubbs was a trustee and the secretary of the Cupar School District, and my first job for him was to transcribe the minutes of the board meeting. When Mr Hubbs moved away I took over the job as secretary and held it for 37 years. I also married a teacher, Miss Annie J. Stuart, on September 29, 1910. We have lived in Cupar ever since.

George E. Penfold
Cupar, Saskatchewan

She remained on the farm working until she was 30 or 31 years old. She did not know that wages were due to her after the age of 16.

When my mother, Margaret Johnson, was six years old, her mother died. Two years later her father took her and her young sister Mary into the Brownlow Hill Institution in Liverpool where, I have found since, he died the following month. Mother was sent soon afterwards to work for a Mrs Hallowell whose husband owned a bake shop. She worked there for five years under very cruel conditions. One day she ran away and found her way back to Dryden Street where she had been born. The neighbours took her in. She was black and blue with whippings. The neighbours then took her to her aunt's home, but unfortunately the delivery boy from the bake shop saw her there and reported it. The authorities from Kirkdale Industrial School came to her aunt's home and took her away. By this time she would be 13 or 14 years old.

The Industrial School then arranged that she would be sent to Canada in May or June 1888. Before sailing, mother remembers that she ran the races that were being held at the school and she won a work box. When her aunt came to the ship to see her off to Canada, mother gave it to her.

Maria Rye was in charge of the party of girls. Mother remembers that there was a storm at sea and they were all afraid. The minister who was on board told them to pray and all would be well.

The children went to the Home at Niagara-on-the-Lake. She does not remember it, but she does remember the little wooden box of clothes with her name 'Maggie Johnson' on it. She went right from the Home to a log cabin on a farm near Rockwood. She did not hear from Miss Rye again. She had not attended school, and probably because of her lack of education, she was afraid to go out anywhere. She remained on the farm working until she was 30 or 31 years old. She did not know that wages were due to her after the age of 16.

Then a lady in the village of Rockwood had a Mr Harvey from Guelph call on her, to ask if she would go to work for them as a servant girl. Mother accepted the offer, and it was there in Guelph a few years later that she met my father—a bricklayer just out from England.

In 1964 my mother and I took a trip back to England and went to the Kirkdale Industrial School. She remembered the rooms and the kitchen where she helped peel potatoes. She also had a reunion with her sister Mary who was then 87. Aunt Mary had been put out to work on a farm in Freshfield, Cheshire, England, at the age of seven. There was another sister and a brother whom we were unable to locate.

Margaret Cleaves, née Johnson
as told by her daughter
Mrs J. R. Bayliss
Brantford, Ontario

THREE

THE YEARS
1900–1904

The night I left for my honeymoon she cried buckets of tears and so did my father whom I adored.

My first recollections of Canada are travelling on the train through Quebec to Montreal. We were sitting three in a seat with the window open. I had a doll and the little girl next to me said 'You know when you get to Canada they will take everything away from you.' 'Well' I said 'They won't get my doll', and I threw it out the open window. I seemed to realize then that I was really alone and I started to cry.

We arrived in Montreal and the next morning we went two by two to St Anne's church to early mass. When we returned we were allowed to play in the back garden until the people came to see us. We were all called inside— 12 boys and 12 girls, and lined up on each side of the room. There were four people there. The woman who was later my adopted mother came over to the little fair girl beside me and said 'I like this one.' My adopted father kept watching me. Every time I looked at him he was smiling at me. He said to my mother 'I like this little dark one' and patted my head. So my mother said 'Well, I guess that's it.' And that is all that was said.

She took my hand and went over to the ladies in charge. They were two unmarried sisters, the Misses Brennan, and the house was in St Anne's Parish, a block or so from the Victoria Bridge. As we crossed over the street my mother asked if I would like to take the street car. I didn't know what she meant, but I thought I would say 'Yes'; it might be something nice. We called street cars 'trams' in Liverpool where I was born.

One other thing stands in my mind about that day I was adopted. There were three little girls—all sisters with me on the train. A man came in a coun-

34

try buggy and took away the two older ones, about eight and ten years, and left the littlest one, four years old, crying on the sidewalk. I have often wondered if she ever saw them again.

The reason I had to come to Canada was because my mother was in the hospital. We were a large family—14 children. My father was a seaman and was away from home on long voyages. So the family was separated and all of us were placed in convents and orphanages.

I came to Canada in May 1900, and I was very lonesome the first year. All summer I had no playmates, and after being with my own large family and then in a convent it was quite a change.

My adopted mother was a possessive person and although she was good to me, I never got too close to her. In England when I would go out with my real mother, she would say 'Hang onto my skirt', as she always had a baby in her arms. So the first time I went out with mother I took hold of her skirt, but she brushed my hand away and said very crossly 'Don't ever do that again.'

She was not outwardly affectionate but I do know she loved me in her own way. The night I left for my honeymoon she cried buckets of tears and so did my father whom I adored. I still have the little Brownie camera that he gave me so many years ago when I was 12.

I was in Canada for five years when the door bell rang one day. We were living in an upper duplex and I leaned over the veranda to see who was there. I saw a young man, 19 years old. He said 'I'm looking for my sister, Annie.' I knew him at once. I ran down the stairs and let him in. My mother didn't think he was my brother, and he had to answer all her questions, and being shy, it was very hard for him. But when my father came home he said that he must be my brother because we looked so much alike. I had four brothers living then and one sister. My brothers were all in the Merchant Marine and came to see me every summer.

I had one brother who came out to Canada before I did. He was sent to Lennoxville, Quebec, to a farm and he was treated very badly and beaten with a strap. After three years he ran away, got to Montreal and onto a ship bound for England. I know of other people, living up around Perth who were taken just to work. They are really broken-down people today, from working hard on farms at 12 and 13 years of age.

My adopted parents had no children of their own. I was well educated and had music lessons. I still play the piano at the Senior Citizens' meetings and my husband sings. My husband and I lived in Montreal for 65 years. After my father died my mother lived with us for nine years, until she died in 1927.

Name withheld by request.

He came at me again. I was scared to death.

My mother died at my birth with my grandmother at her bedside. I was put in the Barnardo Babies Castle until I was two years old and then I was boarded out with a middle-aged lady until I was almost ten.

One day I was taken out of school where I was doing very well and sent to Dr Barnardo's Home at Stepney. I was there about a week when I was shipped out to Canada with about 400 boys and girls. This was in July 1904. All this time I didn't know too well what was going on.

We came to the Toronto Home where Alfred B. Owen was the big guy. I was there about a week, and then I was sent to Reids Mills, a small place outside of Peterborough. I was tired when I got to the place and I didn't know anything about farming. They made me change my clothes and took me out to the barn. I had to climb up the ladder and over a double beam to the loft where I pitched hay.

The next morning the farmer got me up at four o'clock. He had a buggy whip and he yanked me out of bed and gave it to me. I fell down the stairs. He came at me again and I was scared to death. After three months they sent me back to the Home. I thought I was in for more trouble there but nothing happened.

Well, I was in Toronto a few days and they sent me to West Lorne about 40 miles west of London. That was just as bad. I never got any more schooling. I went to the bush and sawed wood and logs. The old man used to beat me for no reason at all. I stuck to it for two and a half years until I couldn't take it any longer. At the time I ran away it was from a beating. I was carrying two big pails of swill for pigs and I had to go through a chicken yard to get to the pigs. I emptied the pails and was returning to the gate—watching the chickens so I wouldn't step on them, they were so thick. All of a sudden I was lying on the ground and he was kicking me in the ribs and whenever he could, he said 'I'll kill you.'

I didn't cry this time. I guess that made him worse. After that I ran away to another farm. The neighbours called Toronto, and the agent from the Home came out and picked up the old man and brought him to the farm where I was hiding. That was the first time I ever saw the agent. He asked me if I wanted to go back with the old man and I said 'No'. So he let me stay on with the other farmer. I did the chores and worked in the garden and finished out my term with the Home. Then, when I was 17, I went out west as far as Saskatoon. I really felt on my own—stayed out there working for eight years. Then I came east again and began work on the railroad in 1925. I worked right through until I was 65 and then I retired. I married in 1954. My wife had five children when she married me—all grown up and they are all good to me and treat me like their father. We have 21 grandchildren and four great-grandchildren.

Harry Jeffery
Essex, Ontario

The cost of his Christmas socks was deducted from his pay.

My father William Gwilliam lived in what he referred to as 'The Home' for four years. His father had died and his mother was unable to look after him and work. She was employed at Witley Court in Shrawley, England, as a maid.

The rules in the Home were strict, discipline harsh, and food scarce. My father begged his mother to let him emigrate. He arrived in Canada in 1902 at the age of 14 with only a shilling to his name. This he promptly spent on apples—something he had always had a craving for. Eventually he planted an orchard in Canada which fulfilled this craving.

He was placed on a farm near Smiths Falls, Ontario. He was not mistreated physically but he was exploited. The summer hour of rising was four o'clock and work continued until dark. The pay was $4.00 a month and board. In the winter the hours were slightly shorter, but there was no pay—only room and board. At Christmas he received a pair of socks. The cost of these was deducted from his pay the following spring.

He spent four years on the farm and then went to the silver mines at Cobalt. He also worked for a winter in the bush of northern Ontario in a lumbering camp.

Those were the days of free enterprise and father was always eager to advance. He saved his money and bought his first farm at Pike Falls, Ontario. The golden opportunity for adventure and advancement next prompted him to sell his farm and go to Moose Jaw, Saskatchewan, where he homesteaded and did very well. He sold out during the 'dirty thirties' and bought another farm near Perth, Ontario. This is where I was born.

Father had a driving ambition. He purchased several other farms in the vicinity and built up a fine herd of Holstein Friesian cattle. To his disappointment all his sons tried farming but left to take jobs in the city. The girls in the family continued on with their education and became—two of us, nurses, two secretaries, and I am a teacher.

Self-reliance, independence and self-discipline were a way of life to my late father. These traits are pretty obvious in our generation also.

William Gwilliam
as told by his daughter
Joyce McGaughey
Long Sault, Ontario

I made a dive out the back door and hid in the turkey hut.

I think I have weathered the storm fairly well to date. I am now 78 years old, and I have been in Canada for 66 years.

I was one of those unfortunate children who came from a drunken father's home. My mother, as I remember faintly, was a handsome woman. She went to an early grave at the age of 32—worn out by drudgery. She left five children behind to fend for themselves. I and my younger sister were placed in Father Banns' Home. We were not Roman Catholic but we were quickly converted to that faith. We were shipped out to this land of rocks and Christmas trees without the knowledge of my father—not that he would have cared.

We landed at Halifax early in May 1904, and came to the St George's Home in Ottawa. From there we were shipped all over Canada to be manhandled by every Tom, Dick and Harry going. My sister came six months before me, at the age of eight. She was placed with a French-Canadian family who ill-treated her. She was then sent to Sussex, New Brunswick, and there she remained until she was of age.

I was 12 when I came, and I was sent on to four farms over the next six years. I was to work until I was 18 for my clothes. Well, talk about the clothes that were given to me to wear. Being an immigrant I was looked down upon as scum. What a transplant—from the slums of London to the misery and loneliness of the backwoods. I had never seen a cow—much less a tomato or potato plant.

I stayed in St George's Home in Ottawa for a few days. Then I was shipped off to the farm by train. I had to change at Coteau for the train to Aubrey. The conductor who was supposed to see me off at Aubrey forgot about me and I landed in Lacolle. The conductor let me pass the night at his dear old mother's home. She wanted to keep me, but in the morning I was on the train again and this time was put off at the right place. I was met by a man from Aubrey. My boss had to work for part of the day and could not meet me, so this man took me to his mother's place for lunch. She gave me my first taste of maple syrup with bread and butter.

At about one o'clock I was driven out to my new place about two miles away from the village. It was a small whitewashed log house. They had one baby boy of 10 months. The man and his wife spoke some English but not much. Being a polite little boy, I kept asking for the water closet. By the time they caught on to what I wanted you can guess I had a few bad minutes. This man was poor. Their food was mostly salted fat pork, potatoes, bread and molasses.

For some reason or another the mistress took a dislike to me. Perhaps I was full of mischief. I do not recall. However I was not an ugly duckling, being fair of skin, curly fair hair, and blue eyes. The farmer worked part time until 11.30 every morning at the milk and cheese factory. It seemed to me that every day when he got home, there was always a tale to be told about me. Although I did not understand the lingo at the time, I sensed the talk was about me at the dinner table.

One fine day I'd had enough and I pointed a finger at her and said 'You, cochon', and I made a dive out the back door and hid in the turkey hut. I don't know if you ever saw one of these. It is triangular so that the hen turkey can go in with her brood to rest out of the rain and wind.

A short time after the boss came out looking for me. He was not able to find me and brought his wife out. Then the neighbours came. They looked all over—in the well, the barn, stables and pigstye. In the meantime I could see all these pairs of legs going by—everyone chattering away. They were getting worried I think, for they were responsible for my welfare. However, I remained on my platform until it started to get dark. The farmer had frightened me with tales of the wild animals in the bush, so I had to come in and face the music. The hut was only about 15 feet from the kitchen door, so in I came. Nothing was said except 'Where were you?' I saw they were relieved when I told them.

No supper that night and off to bed I went. But at three-thirty that morning I was awakened to fetch the horses from pasture, as the farmer left at four o'clock for the factory. You bet I was glad to get back to my raggedy bed after running through the cold dew in my bare feet.

His dear old mother lived some four farms away. She saw that their treatment of me was none too good and she knitted me some black woollen wristlets and gave me a nice soft fur cap for winter. I was told to take them back because they did not want her to dress me. Yet these people were too poor to buy me these articles themselves. In fact they were too poor to buy mortar to fill the cracks between the wooden logs of their house! They had to use cow dung.

The rules of the Home in Ottawa were that I was to attend school until 14. After that I was to get $1.00 a month pay, and they were to feed and clothe me. I did not attend school until fall. I learned nothing, for the teaching was all in French. I was not allowed to visit any neighbours. I never had a ball, sled, skates, or books to read. Not a cent in my pocket until the age of 18. Christmas, New Year's and birthdays meant nothing to them when it came to me. Today, my children ask me why I'm not interested in sports. How could I be?

The first two or three years a man used to come, to ask about my welfare. In later years it was the Sisters of St Vincent de Paul who did this job. I remained at the farm for about a year and a half. By then the farmer saw he could not make a living off the land which was mostly rocks. So he went back to Montreal. I should have returned to Ottawa then, but a farmer had been in touch with the pastor here and wanted me to work for him. The nuns gave permission for me to go.

The food here was somewhat better but not for long enough. The old man, married three times by then, told his wife to get out. The case went to court in Valleyfield, and I was glad when the old lady won. In the meantime I had to be the housekeeper, doing his washing, ironing and cleaning—besides working on a big farm. The son on this farm was about 35 and he was a rotter. I had to go to a neighbour to beg for a stamped form to write home to my folks. If any letters came for me they were opened by this son in the village and read by all before they were given to me. The nuns came to see me and asked that I be given $3.00 per month. The son said I was not worth $3.00. So back I went to Ottawa. I was lucky that I had learned to speak French by then. Don't ask me how much I got from this farmer for the time I slaved for him.

From Ottawa I was sent back to a French farmer who had two big farms at St Clet, and also a forest at St Lazare about eight miles away. I worked there for nearly two years—no doubt for nothing. When the nuns saw the money was not coming I was taken away to Ottawa again. The food was very good, but as elsewhere I was considered an outsider—an immigré d'Angleterre.

In the winter we were up at four o'clock and did the chores before moving off with the team of horses to this bush at St Lazare. Two loads a day—that is what we had to cut and load. Here again I was supposed to be clothed but I got cast-offs from others. In winter the farmer had rubber boots with two pairs of socks. I had leather boots with one pair of socks. I suffered from the cold and I always hated the damn snow.

From Ottawa I was sent to Ontario to an Irish farmer. I think he paid the Home $6.00 a month for me. I was near 18, so I came to Ottawa to claim my fortune. I had written to Father Banns about the nuns having left me to work on some farms without pay. To my surprise the good man thought it his duty to send my letter to the Mother Superior in Ottawa. She wanted me to contradict what I had said but I wouldn't. I told her she could keep my fortune made in six years of labour, but she gave it to me. If I recall correctly it was $70.

I was then on my own. You bet I got away from the farm. I thank the Good Lord for my blessings. I married a girl from here—half Irish and half French—and we have four children. I worked at the Windsor Hotel in Montreal for 47 years. I was laid off in April 1959. I am quite hard of hearing and this, no doubt, was the reason for my dismissal. I was given no pension so it was best to come to this small country hamlet. Not that the cost of living or rents are lower, but it is quiet here and the fresh country air is good to enjoy.

I am not one to believe in the spirit world but in all my tribulations I have always felt my mother by my side.

George Sears
St Chrysostome, P.Q.

The cows came rushing out of the dark and scared the life nearly out of me.

I arrived at this farm after dark. They showed me the pump and told me to start pumping and the farmer would let the cows loose to get a drink. I had never seen a cow before. They came rushing out of the dark and scared the life nearly out of me. That was my first experience in Canada and I will never forget it.

I was eight years old at the time, out from the Strangeways Home in Manchester. I arrived in April 1903 at Mrs Merry's Home in Belleville and went out to the farm.

The people were pretty good to me there, but I had to work hard.

Fred Ashmore
Cardiff, Ontario

My mother became anxious about me and came out to Canada...

My father was far from wealthy and apparently not too healthy. He passed away at the age of 36 when I was six years of age. My mother tried to keep me and my younger brother with her, but it was impossible. For a while she boarded us out so she could work. Finally she suggested to me that I go into a Home. This naturally appealed to a youngster who had been belted around somewhat, so I said 'Yes'. Then away we went, my mother and brother and I down to the Leopold Street branch of the Barnardo Home in London. After all the finality of signing me in, mother and my brother bid me goodbye. Little did I think I was going to be separated from my brother.

After entering the Home I was sanitized so to speak. I was stripped and shot through a large bath—today I think of it as a sheep dip—then over to a counter, where a lady looked over it to see what had been brought in. She sized me up and handed out a new clean wardrobe. So, like a branded animal I was turned out with all the other boys. They were curious to see what the new addition was like and spent a while instructing me in some of the rules of the Home. The regimenting was done mainly by the whistle or a bell—nothing harsh about it.

I remember the first meal. What a din those tin plates and cups made. Then it came time to retire and lights were supposed to be out shortly after. That was the time we got together for a bedside chat, but every once in a while the supervisor would come in and when we saw that ray of light we scrambled for our own beds. I was caught the first night and kindly told not to let it happen again—but it did.

Then the big question was asked. 'How many of you boys would like to go to Canada?' I think about 40 of us wanted to go and get started on farms.

Our parents were notified and their approval secured, so now it was getting our 'portmanteaus' equipped with winter clothes—coat, socks, scarf, and all the rest. I well remember the sight on the dock when the lighter took us out to our ship. Our relatives and friends sang 'God be with you till we meet again.' That was the last I saw of England and my brother. He passed away about a year after I left.

Now, on to Canada, the land of 'milk and honey' as some of us thought. In any event it was better than what we had left. We landed at Quebec the latter part of March, 1901. There we were loaded into trains to head west and fan out in various directions. The coaches were the old-fashioned, slat-seated, and hard-bunked type. I think they were made for immigrants. I was sent to Peterborough where I stayed overnight at the girls' Home called 'Hazel Brae'. I don't remember any other boys stopping there.

The next day I was sent to Keene, Ontario. Nobody was at the station to meet me but the agent told me that the farmer would be after me shortly. While I was waiting I took the notion to kick the telegraph pole just to hear the wires hum—little knowing that at a future date I would be sending messages over those same wires.

It was April 1st, of all days. The farmer finally arrived driving a team of Clydesdale horses hitched to a new farm wagon. He told me to climb in and that seat looked as high up as the cabby's seat on a hansom cab. Up I went. There was not too much said on the way to the farm which was about four miles north of Keene. But the roads were far from smooth, and in those days they were not graded as they are now. We struck one pot hole which deseated me into the bottom of the wagon. The farmer got hold of the neck of my clothes and helped me up on the seat again. We arrived at the farm about supper time.

The farmer very kindly told me to go into the house and get warm. His wife, a former school teacher, bid me welcome and took my overclothes from me. But what really took my fancy more than anything else was the smell of that farm dinner which was cooked and ready for us. It was the first meal of that kind I had ever had and I guess I did it justice. Having a bedroom to myself was really something.

I was to be paid $20 per annum if I stayed five years. This included my keep and the opportunity of going to school in the winter—a three-mile walk. There was a lot of work on the farm. I was introduced to an axe (11 years of age, me), a pile of virgin maple firewood and shown how to split it with the least effort. Some of those blocks weighed as much as I did, but I kept ahead of the woodburning stove, and the boss was satisfied with the progress I was making. Spring ploughing and seeding were all done with horses and I did my share for my age. Threshing was done with the old type of machine, using horse power. I was so fascinated that I watched the threshing instead of the two-year-old youngster I was supposed to be looking after while the farmer's wife was getting things ready to feed the threshers. This provoked her to the point where she thought she was a teacher again, and she ordered me out on the veranda to wait until she was ready for me.

I had an attack of appendicitis which these people thought was a stomach ache, so that I suffered for days before it was decided to get a doctor.

He ordered me to the Sick Children's Hospital but the appendix was not removed. About a year later I had another attack which took me to the hospital again for an operation. My mother, by this time, was anxious about me and she came out to Canada. But she passed away soon after her arrival and this really left me an orphan. I was asked if I wanted to go back to the farm and I said 'No'.

I was sent out to Weston, Ontario, to work for a baker. When he sold out I went across the street to work for a doctor. The baker was to pay me $100 per year, but when I went to work for the doctor, the baker wanted me to send him half of my monthly salary. I immediately wrote to the Home and they told me not to pay. I never did recover the few dollars I had already sent. After a while the new baker wanted me back on account of my knowing the ropes. Remember this was when I was only 13 or 14 years old. Anyway he expected a lot of me and was very cranky, and told me I might as well quit. So quit I did. I worked for a market gardener until December when I was told I was not needed for the winter. I had no home except the Barnardo one, so in I went again.

It was only a few days until another doctor came in looking for a boy. He picked me. You would have thought he was purchasing a horse the way he sized up my forehead, body and legs. Apparently he was satisfied and in a day or two I was sent out to Sunderland, Ontario. I had all manner of jobs to do at this place. Sometimes there were five horses to look after, as well as the rigs. Lots of nights I would have to get up and hitch up a horse and go out with the doctor. I had some pretty cold drives in the winter. Anyway I stuck to this place for seven years. Then I took off and worked on my own.

One day I was reading an ad for a post office clerk and telegrapher. I applied and was accepted. I worked in Gravenhurst about three years, then at Campbellford, Midland, and Seagrave. After 15 years the branch line was due to be closed so I looked around and found that Colborne was open for bids. I was the senior applicant and got the job. I worked for 25 years, until my retirement in 1955.

Today I am enjoying my free time, able to get around, and still drive my car. In July I will celebrate my 88th birthday.

Albert J. Dance
Colborne, Ontario

We wore striped dresses and white hats.

I remember only a few small details of England. I can remember some-one taking me to see the wax works in London. I have no memory of get-ting on the boat, but I do remember being taken with some girls to a big house at Niagara-on-the-Lake around 1904. We wore striped dresses and white hats similar to a sailor's hat with an elastic under our chins. I must have been about six or seven years old. I also remember the church bells at Niagara and we were marched in double line to church on Sundays in charge of a teacher. I never attended a school. We were taught in the Home by a woman teacher and I learned to write and figure—but not very much.

We got oatmeal porridge for breakfast with fruit of some kind (prunes or figs in place of sugar), also bacon drippings for butter but on Sundays or special days we got butter. We were fed quite well, but cheap. The small children did not work but the bigger girls looked after the small ones and also did other chores. Every little while one or two of us would be adopted by someone and we would see them taken away and never see them any more.

I remember the red-coated soldiers coming up around the big house in the evenings and lying around on the grass. They were never allowed inside. The wee girls were allowed to talk to the soldiers but I don't think older girls were.

I must have been there a couple or more years when a woman came one day and took me to Toronto. As I recall, her name was Mrs Sharpe and she was good to me. I can remember standing on a Sunlight soap box to reach the washboard in the tub in her basement to wash clothes. She had two daughters. One was a school teacher, but she never taught me any-thing. I must have been there a couple of years when a Mrs Copeland took me to live with her. No one seemed to have anything to do with where or with whom I lived. I cannot remember anyone ever asking me how I was treated or coming to see me in such a way.

After I was with her some time she would send me to work at some other house for a few days and as time went on I went from one place to another as a maid. I got paid some money after a while and that is what I did as I grew up. When I was doing housework I ran into a girl named Maggie Thompson. In the spring of 1918 she and I came up to visit her sis-ter Mrs Cooper who lived about eight miles from Owen Sound and three miles from Shallow Lake. After a week or so I wanted to stay, so I remained with the Coopers and Maggie went back to Toronto.

Then I went to do housework for a lady on a farm two miles from Shallow Lake. Her husband was a real bad tempered man and one evening after I was there a few weeks, he came in from the barn with two pails of milk and was ugly and threw one pail of milk all over my freshly scrubbed floor. I had a good cry and left there and went to the Coopers.

Then a Mrs Bob Young heard of me and hired me for housework. I was there three months when I went to work in a hotel at Owen Sound, but it got slack in the late fall, and I returned to the Coopers. The night I left the hotel a neighbour of Coopers was taking my trunk out for me when my present husband came along and asked if he could drive me out. I had spoken to him once before; I had to pass his home on my way from Coopers to Shallow Lake. So we went to a picture show and he then took me home. A week or less later he sent me a note by the rural mail asking if he could come to see me. I sent a return note and here I am today.

I stayed at the Coopers that winter. The flu was bad and I did a few days' work here and there where people were sick and also I helped Mrs. Cooper with her four children.

In the spring of 1919 I went to work for a Mr and Mrs Frank McClarity. He was a manager of a wholesale house, and they had a small girl and boy. They were very good to me and took me to the beach with them when they went to live there in June. I got $15 per month which was a good wage at that time. My husband-to-be was allowed into the kitchen through the back door, and I was told to give him a lunch. When I got married on August 20, 1919, I had $45 saved up. The McClaritys gave me a complete suit, hat, shoes, and stockings. After the ceremony we all went to the hotel I had worked at and had our dinner—$1.00 a plate.

I am now 72 and all in all I have had a good life although I did not have a very good start. I often wonder what would have been my fate had I not run into Maggie and had we not gone to visit her sister. Did some divine power control all this? I wonder.

Flora Harrison, née Ward
Owen Sound, Ontario

I would like to see the farm again this spring, but Lord, I am growing old.

Years ago, in 1904, I came to the home of Mr John Senn at Fairview Farm near Caledonia, Ontario. I sailed to Canada on the Victorian. I was an orphan, 14 years old.

I lived in the home of grandfather Senn for five years. I remember him looking at the books I had in my trunk from the Barnardo Home. I used to go with him to church and to Sunday school at York every Sunday. I fed and cared for his pure-bred cattle and worked with his son Mark. I was young then and life was Paradise, never to be lived again. I used to drive the horses and cut wood in the bush with Mark Senn. I never had an accident there in all those years. The bush was about a mile or so from the house and we burnt wood in the stove—and Mark and I used to cut it all. In summer I drove the herd of cattle over a mile to pasture—yes, it would be two miles, as the farm was of considerable extent.

Many times ministers and church people would come to the farm and perhaps stay to supper. In summer we used to catch and spear mullets in the nearby creek and, oh, how Mark used to enjoy that in the spring nights. I knew all the neighbours near by—the Nelles, the Andersons, the Weirs. Often we drove in to York or Caledonia for a few hours. When I look back those seem halcyon days, for I was young and surrounded by the happiest of circumstances.

I left the farm after six years and joined up for World War I. I served for three years and was captured after most of us in our battalion were wounded or killed. After the war I returned to Canada, taking one of my sisters with me to Montreal where we each got a situation. I worked for 25 years at the Montreal General Hospital and at various other places. I had no schooling in Canada, but I had about eight years in England before I came here.

I would like to see the farm again this spring, but Lord, I am growing old, though I believe I could still make the journey. I still remember how we used to drive in to church at York and how we used to have a Bible reading and prayer in the morning following our breakfast. I had then what is far more precious than wealth. I had youth and the God-given vitality that only youth has. It is strange that in all that hell of Passchendaele and even in the prisoner of war camp I never feared life as I do now in easy circumstances and safety. It seems a paradox, but it is not.

The remembered and dear faces are all gone now, and sometimes I feel as if the flame of my life has left me and I am just a shell. But my good memories are a blessed thing.

Richard Jack
Montreal, Quebec

*It was me up first in the morning to start a fire in the kitchen stove,
put on the kettle and then go out to feed the sheep a big armful of
rough hay.*

In 1904 my brother and I, Ellen Keatly, were put in the Middlemore
Home in Birmingham by our father; the following year we were sent to
Nova Scotia. I was about nine when we landed at Scotsburn station in
Pictou County, after riding the train from Halifax, this being the nearest
station to where we were to live. The two farmers came with a horse and
buggy each to get us. We had tags on the front of our coats like bags of
potatoes. Scotsburn is 10 miles from Loganville and 10 miles from the
town of Pictou.

The people I lived with in Loganville were Scotch, named Baillie.
Major Baillie was away a lot. Being a Pipe Major, he went to Aldershot for
two weeks when the soldiers were training at camp. The son, Sandy, was a
year or two older than me. We went to school near by and played together. With Major Baillie being away Mrs Baillie and us children had to get in
the hay and grain, look after the vegetables and animals—about five or six
milking cows and some young cattle, sheep, a pig, turkeys, chickens and
ducks. Major Baillie built a hen house to hold about 110 hens soon after I
was there. I soon learned to milk with Mrs Baillie helping. They had a
cream separator, and made butter with a dasher churn. There was no water
in the house so I had to carry most of what we used from a river downhill
about 100 yards. It was a hard climb, winter and summer.

There was a bridge over the river and the school was just past it. As
I was the nearest scholar it was me who went early to light the wood fire.
I was paid $2.00 for doing that all winter, and I had to find the kindling.
It was me up first in the morning to start a fire in the kitchen stove, put on
the kettle, then go out to feed the sheep a big armful of rough hay. They
were closed in a small corner of the barn so had to be let out. When I came
in Mrs Baillie had tea ready and was cooking porridge. After the tea we
went out to the barn and milked and fed the cows. The horses were fed and
watered so as to be ready for Sandy and his dad to plough or haul lumber.
After having my porridge the pig was fed and all the fowl. That meant
more water to carry; I even had to run home at recess to carry water. Sandy
and I had to saw wood in our spare time to keep the fires going in winter;
and wood fires burn out in the night so the house got very cold. This had
been a large frame boarding house for workers at Logan's Tannery nearby.
The tannery burned down before I arrived.

The country was beautiful around there—so much woods and hills. We could look up and see Dalhousie Mountain from the house. The Baillies were good musicians. Mrs Baillie could play a small set of bagpipes and she taught Sandy and other young fellows to play. She was from Inverness, Scotland. Her father, Alexander McLennan, was a great piper; he had played before Queen Victoria. Major Baillie had come to Canada as a young child with his parents. He joined the British Army as a young man and had a pension from it. He was a good violin player and Mrs Baillie also played the piano.

With all the cold and hard work I enjoyed life. I will say that there was always plenty to eat. They killed a pig and beef animal for winter meat. Mrs Baillie had a spinning wheel brought from Scotland. She spun wool from the sheep. It had to be sent to a carding mill to be made into bats. It was the thing then to get enough stocking legging cut from a roll at the general store, then pick up the stitches on four knitting needles and knit feet of natural wool which had been spun on the wheel. We had leather boots and to make them waterproof we greased them often with melted tallow or fat. The men wore larrigans made waterproof with tallow.

I wasn't beaten or abused. Major Baillie was kinder to me than his wife was. Once he took me to his brother's home at Earltown for two nights. That was the only time away from the farm for eight years. There was a gathering of farm people. He played the pipes for them. Once, the Major, his wife, and Sandy went to a Highland gathering in Prince Edward Island. By this time Sandy was able to play the pipes with his father. I had to do all the chores and stay alone for two nights. We used oil lamps and I remember being nervous as it got dark and I lit them. The lady on the next farm came to see me one evening.

In 1913 I left the Baillies. I was finished with school and tired of the hard work, no money, and very few clothes. I was advised to write to the home at Fairview near Halifax. Mr King was the head of the place and he came to the Baillies with the mail driver. I packed in a hurry. Sandy drove us to the station to go on the train to Pictou where I stayed in a hotel. The next morning we got a train to Halifax. I stayed at the Home for about two weeks, then went to Rockingham on Bedford Basin to live with the Fielding family. This seemed so nice after the farm. I helped with the washing and cleaning and got to know a bit about cooking. I was paid $5.00 a month. There was another Home girl placed a few doors from me. Her name was Annie Newton. She had had a hard life with a farmer in Cape Breton. We got to be close friends and were allowed to take the train in to

Halifax to go to movies and do shopping. Then we both got jobs at house-work with more pay in the city. Then I met the man I married and settled here in 1918.

Ellen Higgins, née Keatly
Brantford, Ontario

Then I said 'Good night, Madam' and she left.

I well remember the first night I slept away from home. We were taken first to a very wealthy British home. The lady of the house put us to bed. When she turned to leave she said 'Good night'. I said 'Good night'. She stood at the door and looked at me for a minute or two. Then I said 'Good night, Madam', and she left.

My father died when I was six or seven years old, so my mother put two of her boys in the Barnardo Home. My brother was ten and I was eight when we came to Canada in 1902. We landed in the home of an elderly widow, and we were there together for two years. Then we were separated, but not far apart. We visited each other quite often. My brother joined the army in World War I. When he came back I was married and he lived with us until he died and I buried him in our cemetery in 1924.

I worked on the Canadian National Railway for 37 years and during that time I served as a part-time minister in the Brethren in Christ Church. In 1957 our church went into the pastoral system and I was elected pastor and served for nearly 10 years. I am now retired with many pleasant experiences to remember.

Rev. Wm Charlton
Stevensville, Ontario

FOUR

THE YEARS
1905–1908

We were only Home boys.

I am one of those emigrant boys that came to Canada in 1907 on the White Star Line. I landed at Halifax about March 22. We went to the Brockville Home and were there for two weeks—100 of us boys. We were the cheapest slave labour the farmers ever had.

I was wondering how you got to even thinking of such people as us. I thought we were long forgotten as we were only Home boys and it didn't matter much about what happened to us. We were of no importance.

George Mackie
Pembroke, Ontario

He had a variety of canes from three to five feet in length hidden behind his books.

I well remember the day my father took me to the Barnardo Home at Stepney Causeway. I knew a few weeks in advance that this was going to happen but I never knew why. My father said at one time that he would tell me but he never did. I presume he did not want me roaming the streets of London and getting into trouble.

Upon admission, I was given a complete clean-up. I was dirty and lousy as a pet coon. I was issued clean clothing and boots. All the boys wore sailor suits and caps. The smaller boys wore knee-length pants, and the older ones had the bellbottomed type.

Soon I was taken to the Home at Epsom. There were 100 of us in that institution, ranging in age from about five years to grown-up young men.

When I went there I was the smallest, and upon leaving 16 months later, I had moved up to fourth place at the meal table. Each boy was placed at the table according to his height.

One thing we received was lots of sleep. Each boy had his cot, and he was in it with the lights out at six o'clock. We were up at six in the morning and no second calling. We rose and got dressed, went to the washroom and had hands and face washed, usually by an older boy. Then to breakfast. When it came time for school we were marched out navy style. We had one teacher who was a regular hell-cat. On Monday morning she would greet us 'Good morning, boys, and let's see who will be the first to get the cane.' It would not be long before some luckless fellow would be rapped over the knuckles. She was eventually brought up on the carpet and discharged for unmercifully beating one of the boys.

On Sunday some of the boys were taken to church. One Sunday I went to sleep in church—a trait I never did get over right into my teens. The matron informed the master, and I was invited up to his study and received an application of the cane (minus the sugar) on my hands. He had a variety of canes from three to five feet in length hidden behind his books.

After one year and four months in the Home, I was included with the party of boys headed for Canada. We arrived in Quebec City on July 1, 1905. On the farm I was not subject to abuse, but was I kept under very strict control! I was not allowed to indulge in any playtime activities which might jeopardize the responsibilities of my 'foster parents'. I started at $5.00 per month. They fed and clothed me, and sent me to school, church, and Sunday school, and gave me as many chores as I was physically capable of handling.

The supervision of children by the Home was a big job—too many children and not enough staff to investigate. As a rule someone came around about twice a year.

I stayed with the family for my term of five years and in the fifth year I received $75, and bought my own clothing, such as it was. At the end of the sixth year I received $100. By that time I wanted a change, so at 19 I left and went on my own.

In all, I worked 57 years in Canada, and retired from the job of marine engineer aboard a Great Lakes freighter. My wife has passed away. Now I do my own housework, some cooking, and sometimes I eat out.

Ernest A. C. Gould
Hamilton, Ontario

That German language was right down my alley.

When I landed in Canada around June 1, 1908, I had very little education, because I had been moved to different boarding places by the Dr. Barnardo Homes. Our first stopping place after we arrived in Canada was the branch office in Toronto. I was eleven years old.

I got placed about a week later on a farm near the village of Tavistock, Ontario, and stayed with one farmer for four and one-half years. The first two winters I went to school for four months and the next one for three months. That was the extent of my schooling. I was in senior third class.

The farmer sold out so I was more or less on my own. I worked on various farms until September 1915 when I enlisted in World War I, and the following month I was overseas. I was invalided back to Canada in 1918.

I would be remiss if I didn't say anything of those beautiful years in the county of Oxford. The north end was quite a mixture of those of German descent. Some churches were all German language, and the church I attended, Zion Evangelical, had German in the morning and English at night. That German language was right down my alley. Before I was in Canada six months I could speak, read, and write both the High German and the Low Pennsylvania Dutch, which was the language used by the Mennonites who were mostly Hamish. I won prizes for speaking the language fluently, and when I was in the army I was called on to interpret.

I was married in 1918 and we had a son and a daughter. I retired in 1964 and am enjoying the autumn of life.

Thomas Wharf
London, Ontario

All jobs were paid at the rate of $1.00 a day and board, and carry your own blankets.

In April 1907 I was called into a conference of the family. I was 15 years old, nearly six feet tall and weighed 160 pounds—pretty skookum. They asked me how I would like to go out to western Canada and help to open up the country. Well, after reading all the books of that time about the Golden West—full of Indians, cowboys and Mounties I naturally agreed. Who wouldn't, at that age?

I was born in Broughty Ferry, now a suburb of Dundee, Scotland, on November 1, 1891. My father died when I was a young child, and my mother had to go to work. I spent my early childhood with my grandparents. In those years attendance at school was the law until the age of fourteen, but an exemption could be made to let a boy leave if he had to go to work. I got that exemption to help out at home.

I have no knowledge of who was responsible for the emigration of young people at that time. I only know that as far as I was concerned the orders were to sail from Glasgow on May 4, 1907, on the Cassandra for Quebec, and to report to the immigration office at Edmonton, Alberta. I had to have 10 shillings on arrival for food on the train to the West.

My mother took me to Glasgow by train. We stayed overnight and she saw me off on the ship next morning. It was loaded with immigrants— mainly Ukrainian. None spoke English. After a rough voyage of 10 days, steerage, we arrived at Quebec, and got on the train for Edmonton. When we reached our destination seven days later, I was pretty well broke. My 10 shillings had disappeared for food. At Edmonton, I was put on a train for Fort Saskatchewan where I was met by a Scottish farmer. I was told that I would stay with him for one year for board and work clothes—no wages— and the next year, I would get a small wage. The idea was apparently to learn the ways of the country and take a homestead.

I stayed at that first place for three months. I found I was doing all the work and the owner was hitting off 14 miles into town every morning and back at night, leaving me to do everything. I went on my own and worked on ranches, at mule-skinning, and on building the railroads which were going out all over the West at that time. It was really tough going. All jobs were paid at the rate of $1.00 a day and board, and carry your own blankets. I roamed the West for seven years until 1914 when war broke out. I enlisted in Regina and spent the next four and a half years as a sergeant in the Canadian army in France and Belgium.

I started police work in Regina in 1919, and continued with the Royal Canadian Mounted Police for 40-odd years on the prairies. While I was stationed at Russell, Manitoba, in 1928, there was a large farm just out of town with big buildings—then deserted. It had been a training centre for Dr Barnardo's boys prior to 1914. I ran across quite a few of the old Barnardo boys in that area who had learned farming at the settlement and who had taken their own homesteads. Some were quite wealthy.

I feel it has been a privilege to have had a hand in opening up the country. I am happy now to just sit back and watch the world go by. This is a, lovely country in the Gulf Islands. Spring flowers all in bloom and temperatures up in the 50s day and night.

Dave J. Brims
Gabriola Island, British Columbia

The next place...was owned by a beast.

My husband died in September 1961. I can only tell you his story as he told me. On his birth certificate it states that he was born July 18, 1897, at the Union Workhouse. His mother was a laundress at Torquay. His father's name is only a dash. At one time we were told by the representative at the Barnardo Home that his mother kept him for three years and then had to put him in a Home, for she was in poor health and died shortly after. Another time they told us not to be unduly anxious as he had made a good life in Canada. What a farce that statement was to my husband.

He came to Canada when he was eight and was sent to a home near Dunnville, Ontario, to be with an elderly lady. He was only with her a very short time, but she was a mother to him and he worshipped her. This was the only place where he had any steady schooling and what you would call a home. Unfortunately she had a fire in her little three-roomed house and she had to be put in a Home. So that was the end of my husband's world for a number of years.

The next place he was sent to was owned by a beast who used to beat his wife and my husband whenever he was drunk and that was often. Finally he ran away but they found him and took him back for more beatings. I don't know where he went from there. He used to speak of another place where the husband was all right but the wife was a devil. He told me many things. It seems unbelievable that our society let such things go on. And the representative surely knew. It seemed to my husband that the farmers knew when the representative would be coming around and would send him out to the barn or way down by the creek and tell him not to come until they called.

My husband was very bitter. I have seen him break down when he told me some of the stories, and it is hard to see a man do that. Thank God we had a happy life together.

William Wood
as told by his wife, Ellen Wood
Kitchener, Ontario

He was only 15 years old when he went to Heaven to rest.

I was six years old in the year 1907, and too small to help on the farm. My father wanted a bigger man. So he made some kind of an arrangement with people representing Dr Barnardo's Home, as it was called.

And so in a year or so he got word that a shipload of boys would be coming out to Canada. My father was given the chance to pick the one he liked. He picked out a fellow 12 years old by the name of Arthur James Dare. He was a welcome member of our family and lived amongst us. We went to school together.

But he didn't stay very long. Only until he was 15 years old, and then he went to Heaven to rest. Now he is all forgotten. He left behind a Bible with Dr Barnardo's photograph in it. A few years ago I put a piece in the paper that anybody from the Home could have his Bible—first come, first served—but nobody ever called.

After that I wrote a letter to the Home calling for some relative of his to write to me in the name of friendship, because he was my friend. But there was no answer—no trace of him at all. I have a picture of him yet.

Arthur James Dare
as told by his friend, Com Falk
Grunthal, Manitoba

I saw this boy who looked familiar. I walked up to him and said 'I think you're my brother.'

Dr Barnardo was at the ship to bid us farewell when my brother David and I sailed for Canada in 1905. David was nine and I was eleven. I remember that we were in the back of the ship, probably third class. The voyage lasted between two to three weeks. We were stopped for at least one day by icebergs.

On our arrival in Canada we went by train to Winnipeg and spent about two weeks together in the Home. There we were told we would be separated. I remember we crawled into bed together that last night and cried with our arms around each other until we went to sleep.

I was sent to a farmer near Miniota, Manitoba. One day about three years later my boss took me to a country fair. I was wandering around and I saw this boy who looked familiar. I walked up to him and said 'I think you're my brother.'

When my boss came to say it was time to go home, I said 'I've found my brother.' So he gave us two bits and told us to go and buy something with it. We bought some bananas and sat on the railway ties and talked and talked. My brother lived at Beulah, a village about nine miles north from my place.

My brother David was awarded a medal from the Barnardo Home for Good Conduct and Length of Service.' I did not receive one. I was moved from my first farm, although I did not tell the Home representative of my plight. The hired man wrote to someone about it—probably to the Home—and I was moved to another place where I stayed until my brother and I went overseas in 1914.

Alex McKean
Miniota, Manitoba

The following extract regarding the admission of the McKean boys is from the Barnardo Home records:

Full agreement with Canada clause assigned by sister [of Mrs McKean] Mrs Mary Ann Gilmore. These orphan boys have been admitted on application of Miss E Purvis, lady superintendent of the Nursing Association, Middleborough, who filled out a question form supplying the following information:

Father, McKeen, [sic] was foreman at the Middleborough gasworks and died two years ago from the result of an accident. The relatives are mostly decent, hardworking people who have a good reputation in the town but none of them are very well off. We are not told how the mother maintained herself after her husband's death. She became broken down in health and for some months was under the care of the district nurse, her sufferings at times being very severe. It is said that a more patient or gentle woman a nurse never had. It had been her great wish that the boys be sent to Dr Barnardo and when the promise was given, she said 'I am glad, now I can die happy. My poor boys will be cared for.' Her death took place on 18 October, 1899.

The relatives were all anxious that the boys should be admitted and propose sending annually a small sum to the Home towards their support. The boys are certified to be in excellent health. They have had measles.

Those seven years were hell.

From 1905 to 1970 is a long time and I can't remember whether it was Montreal or Halifax where we landed in August 1905. We went first to Toronto and then on to Winnipeg. I was only overnight at both these Homes. Then I was sent out to Arrow River in Manitoba where I was put on contract to this farmer for seven years. When my time was over he had to deposit $130 in a bank for me.

Those seven years were hell. I was beat up with pieces of harness, pitchforks, anything that came in handy to hit me with I got it. I didn't get enough to eat. I had to drink water for my meals and they had eight cows milking. I herded cattle for five years—no horse, no dog—nothing to tell the time by. I had to have the cattle home by 5.30 in the afternoon. If I was late I got beat up. My dinner was put up in a 10-pound syrup pail. Not wrapped—just a piece of paper to cover it. When it was time to eat it, it was as dry as old toast. I used to eat it as soon as I got out of sight of the house in the morning. I used to swipe flour and sugar. I judged the time by the neighbours and when noontime came I used to take my dinner pail and get milk from the cows and make flour porridge.

I never had a coat if it was raining. Just a grain sack over my shoulders and no shoes. I was supposed to go to school six months of the year, and in the seven years I only got to grade three. We had a slate and pencil and a scribbler made out of brown wrapping paper and sewn down the middle.

We had three miles to walk to church, and I was supposed to go every Sunday. I only went in winter because I was herding cattle in the summer. They would buy me shoes that wouldn't fit. I used to cry with the pain. My feet are still crippled over that. They also used to buy me one-fingered mitts for the winter and if one got wore out they would make me a mitt from an old sock. They made my underwear from grey flannelette. It did not keep out much cold. I used to have to bucksaw all the wood for the fires. It did not matter if it was 40 below, I had to be out sawing wood and splitting it. I used to go in to get warm but if I stayed too long I got a licking. I had to pitch sheaves with grown-up men and I had to keep my turn. So, as I said, they were seven years of hell. I had some good jobs after that.

The year I married—1920—my wife and I worked on a farm. I got $30 a month and she got $10 a month with room and board. It was a good place.

My wife passed away in 1962. I have four boys and two girls. I live alone on my old-age pension of $111.41 a month. I pay $30 a month for my room and I board myself. I am far from being all right as far as my health goes.

Charles W. Carver
Winnipeg, Manitoba

*I thanked them for the gifts—thought it was grand. Guess the
answer I got.*

I arrived in Bromley township, Ontario, in April 1908 just before my
15th birthday. I was lonesome and I cried up in the hay mow. Then about
the middle of June, while I was milking cows, the farmer began to talk
strange to me. I did not understand at first what was wrong. He was asking
me how much money I had in my box, and I said I had one shilling—
brought out from the Quarrier Home. Then he asked me what I had done
with the $35 that was stolen. He promised he would not tell the Home if
I told him. Just think—six weeks in a strange country and asked about a
stolen $35. I was brokenhearted—I didn't even know what a dollar bill
looked like. Near Christmas the daughter of the house told me that her
mother had found the money in her raincoat pocket. So you can judge for
yourself what happened.

That year from the Christmas tree, I got rubber boots, socks, and mitts.
I felt so happy about it. I thanked them for the gifts—thought it was grand.
Guess the answer I got.

'Oh, you're paying for everything' he said.

He had to pay me once a year. In those five years I received about a dol-
lar a year. The year I was seventeen, I got 30 cents for the year, and then
they charged me 15 cents for a hair cut. His wife cut it.

I was the cause of the horse running away with the rake—worth $5.00.
I allowed him $10 from my wages towards it, not knowing at the time—
now get this—that the Home Inspector had told him not to raise my wages
because of the rake. So it just cost me $22. The farmer then bought a new,
all-steel rake for $26. You didn't get much chance to speak to the Home
Inspector about what was going on.

Another time I bought a watch from the farmer for $4.00. I guess it
cost him 50 cents. Later he told me he had charged me $8.00 for it because
he had thrown in a chain. The chain was tied in the middle with a cotton
thread. I could have gotten a better one in Woolworths for 10 cents.

Then one summer I went to a picnic, walked eight miles with 50 cents
pocket money. Left the picnic early, was picked up part way home and arrived
just after supper. I said I'd had no supper and he said 'I don't feed you when
you're away all day.' Once I asked him to take me to Douglas. Hadn't been to
town in 14 months, and his answer to that was I'd lose half a day's pay. I blew
my top at that. He swore at me and I did the same, and I walked out on him.

Anyway, when I left Douglas, he took me to the station. He said if I
needed a job I would know where to come. I have made my mistakes, but

I'm happily married and have no regrets now. His grandchildren couldn't be better to us. My wife and I just love them all. I was a little scared about writing this account because I wouldn't hurt those grandchildren for anything.

Jack Saunders
Toronto, Ontario

They'd squirt tobacco juice all over the stove. It would hiss and the kids would giggle, and the teacher would blow her top.

I was born in Rochester, Kent, England, in May 1895, so I'm no chicken, eh? My father was a teller—a keeper of cargo records—on the steamer City of Rochester which carried coal between Newcastle and the towns on the Medway River in Kent. He took a stroke on board the boat, lingered on for a week, then passed away in March 1903. Well, it was pretty rough for mother with us two boys and a baby in the cradle. That is the sole reason for us boys going into the Barnardo Home. Mother could not make ends meet. There was only a little charity in those days. I can still remember my brother and me taking a clean pillow slip and going to an old folks' home where they filled it up with bread for us. Yes, it was tough pickings in those days.

Mother said she often regretted putting us in the Home. She and my uncle tried to get us out, but they would have had to pay for our keep for four months. They did not have that kind of money. So eventually when my brother Ernest was seven and I was ten, we came out to Canada.

There was a large party of boys—I cannot say how many, but we had a train to ourselves going from the Home down to Liverpool. The Barnardo Boys' Band came with us and I will always remember when the boat was pulling away from the dock. They played 'God be with you till we meet again'. Every time I hear that hymn, it brings back vivid memories.

We had a fair trip—games on deck and cocoa and biscuits before turning in at night. We saw some whales spouting water, and a couple of icebergs. We reached Quebec City safely on July 1, 1905, and heard a lot of strange bells. They were the railway trains. We crossed the St Lawrence on a large ferry to Levis, Quebec, and entrained for Toronto. The Home there served as a distributing centre. There were six of us boys sent to Lowbanks Station eight miles east of Dunnville, Ontario. Two of them, I never saw again, but my brother and I went to the same farmer (a Mr Kirby) and the other two boys went to the same country school so we were often together. That was some school. A one-room frame school house with a big box stove for heating. The older boys just went to school in the winter months. They used to fire up the stove with cordwood. Teacher would yell 'Don't make so much noise'. They'd say 'O.K. Main', and then squirt tobacco juice all over the stove. It would hiss and the kids would giggle, and the teacher would blow her top.

My brother and I were at Kirby's for over two years on the boarding-out system. We were to help around with the chores after school and the farmer got $60 per year for keeping us. He had to supply board and some clothing.

Then Mr Kirby moved to New York State, and we were not allowed by the Home to go with him, being under age. My brother was sent to a farm about three-quarters of a mile from the farm where I was sent. By this time I was old enough to start working steady so I started on a five-year term of hiring out. The first year I got my board and clothes and the second year I got the same plus $10 for the year. The cash amount went up $10 each year—totalling $100 for the five years of work.

During the last summer we were clearing up new ground. We set fire to some brush piles. The wind came up and blew embers over into the bush and set it afire. We tried to check it by making fire-breaks, but it got the best of us. We could not get it out. But luckily a heavy thunderstorm came up through the night, and got it under control. Boy, it sure scared me.

After I finished my farm term I came in to Welland and worked in a couple of factories. When World War I broke out, we joined up and went overseas to France and Belgium. That was where I lost my brother. He was killed at Vimy Ridge on April 9th, 1917, and I sure have missed him.

Looking back, I can say that the opportunities in England did not excel those here. But if I had not gone into the Home, my future would have been anyone's guess.

Percy F. Mitchell
Port Colborne, Ontario

They put me in a cell at the head of the stairs and all the prisoners coming in from the jail farm stared at me.

I was born in Belfast, Ireland, on June 4, 1898. When my mother died in February 1907 my aunt took my two sisters, and my brother and I were left with my father. My father was a labourer and away at work all day so that we two boys ran a little wild, but nothing serious. The climax came when the authorities inquired why we were missing school.

They were strict in Belfast about school attendance. My father was hauled into court with us two boys to explain our absence. He told them about his situation and we boys made all kinds of promises to help him, including selling papers. But the promises were soon forgotten and selling papers became tiresome. Again father was notified that we were missing school. He took several days off and escorted us to the school door. There was a long corridor running through the building with four rooms opening off it. When father took us to school he would see that we went in the front door and he would stand there until the bell rang. In the meantime we went straight down the corridor and into the back yard. We would climb the wall around the grounds and lie down behind it and wait until father left. Then we would take off and play the rest of the day. So once again we were taken into court. This time the judge told father that he would have to put us into an institution or we would end up in reform school.

Eventually in the fall of 1907 my brother and I were placed in the Barnardo Home in Belfast. My brother had heard great stories of the wealth to be gained in Canada and wanted to come here. But I wanted to join the navy. At that time Britain used to take boys of 10 into the navy and train them as midshipmen.

I stubbornly insisted on the navy for some two months, and held up the decision to send us to Canada. Of course my father was reluctant too, to let us go so far away. He met us several times coming from school and we discussed it with him. Eventually, with pressure from my two sisters, my brother, and a very militant aunt, I gave in and agreed to come to Canada. So after Christmas in 1907 we were sent to Clapham in London and were shipped out from there in March 1908. We were 13 days on the ocean, and as near as I can remember we travelled to Winnipeg in those old railway cars with the wooden seats.

Naturally my brother and I hoped to be kept together but the morning after we arrived at Winnipeg he was sent to a farm at Theodore, Saskatchewan, and I was sent to a bush farm at Lavalle in northern Ontario. I never saw him again until I met him in France, behind Vimy Ridge nearly 10 years later. Apparently the people at Theodore had been good to him and he still keeps in contact with the family today.

I, on the other hand, had a harsh master who often used the black snake whip on me. While I was working for this man I had to get up at five o'clock in the morning and do the chores—such as milking the cows and feeding the calves, pigs and chickens—before I walked three miles to school. I often had to scrub floors, wash dishes, and mind the babies—all of which did me no harm and, I believe, made me better fitted to face life. In winter I sawed wood with a cross-cut saw and piled cordwood after school hours and on Saturdays and holidays.

In summer I cleared land and hauled and piled roots with a jersey bull hitched to a stone boat. One morning, while gathering the eggs I saw something white moving ahead of me as I crawled from one manger in the barn to another. I became frightened and ran into the house—and being an ignorant city boy, I called out that there was a snake in one of the mangers. The boss came back with the rifle and shot a skunk.

Another time I was coming down the corduroy road a half mile from home. I saw a small dark animal on the edge of the road. It would eat a while and then sit up and look around. I was afraid to pass it, and threw sticks but it wouldn't move. I'd heard much talk of beavers and I thought it was one. So I went around it and ran home to tell them that there was a large beaver up the road. The boss got his rifle and came back with me. He looked around and showed me bear tracks, and told me I was very lucky that I hadn't hurt the cub or the old mother would have been after me.

Later on, in 1930, I went to see my boss. He was then the caretaker of a large school at Fort Frances, Ontario. He had children grown up then— the children I had looked after and held on my knee. He apologized for the way he had treated me. He said that if he'd known as much then as he did now that he was old, he would have treated me different.

In 1912 I hired out to an old army captain on a farm near Portage la Prairie, Manitoba. He was a veteran of the North West Rebellion. After six months I wanted to leave, and he refused to let me go. He said I had a contract and if I broke it he would put me in jail. This was a challenge, so I left. Just outside town he caught up to me with the horse and buggy. He told me he was going to get the police and have me arrested so I got into the buggy with him and drove to the police station. I held the horse while he went in and talked to the police. When he came out he sent me in to speak to the chief. The chief tried to persuade me to go back and when I refused the police arrested me. They took me to the provincial jail and put me in a cell at the head of a flight of stairs and all the prisoners coming in from the jail farm stared at me as they went past. I found out next day that I had been in the cell for condemned prisoners.

When I was returned to court a week later, there sitting in the front row was the representative of the Barnardo Home from Winnipeg. I was released and returned with him. About three days later he sent me out to a Scottish immigrant family. I stayed with them a year until they talked about signing adoption papers and then I left. I didn't want to be tied up with anyone. I worked around on farms in Manitoba until February 1916 when I was accepted into the army and went overseas with the Canadian Expeditionary Force. I served in France for 15 months, took part in five important battles, was wounded twice—the last time on the second day of the big breakthrough at Amiens.

After the war I worked on construction and road building for a year and a half. Then I joined the Canadian National Railway as a fireman and worked until 1928 when I was put out by the railway union as an organizer for four years. In the 30s I was laid off. I could have gone back to work on the Hudson Bay railroad which was then being built, but I had married in February 1927 and had a young wife, so I refused the job.

I had a small pension for war disabilities and with the small bush farm I bought we managed O.K. In 1940 I joined the army and after serving for six years, I went to the federal government in Middlebro. Now I am retired.

Matthew Clarke
Middlebro, Manitoba

THE YEAR
1909

I will never forget that house on the Lakeshore Road—the flickering shadows on the wall from the oil lamps and the creaking and cracking of the frost on those dark, cold, winter nights.

I was about eight when I was placed in the Fegan Home, and I was sent to Canada when I was 10. The Fegan Home was situated at Stony Stratford, Buckinghamshire, some distance north of London. There were no women that I could see. We were ruled by what, for the most part, were hard masters. I guess they were pretty much a law unto themselves. We slept in large dormitories and if we did not hear the signal to get up, our cots were tipped over and we were on the floor. We ate in a large dining hall at rows and rows of long tables. We took our plates to one end of the room and our food was given to us as we passed along.

Friday night was bath night. We were divided into groups and sent into a large tank. When we came out, we were inspected for cleanliness and then we lined up for clean clothes. Sometimes they fit. While there was not much work to do, we were sometimes made to scrub the dormitory floor, which was pine. We would start in a row with scrubbing brushes and work our way from one end to the other.

Sometimes we would polish brass doorknobs and knockers, and once in a while we would be spread out across a soccer field to pick up everything there was in the grass. Once in a while a boy would run away and we would walk around the playground wondering if he would be caught. He always was, of course, and he would be thrashed before a full assembly—I imagine to put the fear of the Lord in our hearts. He would be beaten across the bare buttocks with a strap or a rubber-soled sneaker. Then he would be put on bread and water for so many days and would not receive any pocket money for some time. At mealtime he was made to stand on the platform, where all the boys facing that way would see him.

Every so often, it might have been once a month, we had what was called 'Judgement Day'. We boys went one by one into a room where all the masters were and they would judge us. The grade they gave determined the amount of pocket money we would receive, and other privileges. We had a good music teacher who taught us breath control, and all the fundamentals of singing. We had a choir and on occasion we would be sent to revival meetings held in tents. I never knew who was holding the meetings, but I have since thought it might have been Billy Sunday.

In April, 1909, a group of us were sent to London. We were given small trunks with our names on them for our clothes. Then we went to Liverpool and boarded the Empress of Britain. We came steerage and everything was pretty crude, but for a group of small boys, I guess it was quite an adventure. When we arrived at Saint John, New Brunswick, we boarded the old wooden immigrant cars. It was a horrible trip to Toronto. We wondered about all those pails tied to the trees. We had never heard of maple syrup.

After a few days in Toronto, I was sent to Oakville to live with two maiden ladies. They lived on the outskirts of Oakville, on what I think would be the Lakeshore Road. Their house was well back from the road, and their property ran down to Lake Ontario. I think that their family was quite prominent at one time. I saw oil paintings of some of their ancestors hanging in the rooms.

I used to bring in fuel, cut the grass and weeds, and look after the chickens. I had my meals in the same room with them but not at the same table. When they finished eating they would go into another room, and I would clear the table and wash the dishes. I will never forget that house— the flickering shadows on the wall from the oil lamps and the creaking and cracking of the frost on those dark, cold winter nights. I really knew what it was to be afraid and a good many nights I cried myself to sleep.

Sometimes I would be taken to Oakville. A livery would be sent out for us. I can still see Miss Susan lifting her veil to taste the butter to make sure it was all right.

I was in Oakville for a year, and then I was put on a train and sent to Darlington station. I don't know how everything was arranged, but someone must have watched over me and put me off at the right station. A farmer was waiting for me with a team of horses. My trunk was loaded on and the farmer drove to his home. He had a wife and three children, the boy being about 12. This was an improvement over Oakville, but I realized my function was to work. When I was in the fields working I could see all the children going to school with their lunch pails. The feeling of utter loneliness would be hard to describe. The farmer had a very bad temper and at times his wife and daughter would act as a buffer and make things easier for me. I received $36 a year at this farm, and I had to buy my clothes out of that. Of course everything was very cheap at that time. In the second winter it was arranged for me to go to school for six weeks. I was placed in grade four, and that was the extent of my education. I stayed at this place for two years, and then moved to another farm where everything was about the same.

The third farm I went to belonged to a rich, city-bred man. He purchased it to place his son who was quite erratic. He thought farm life might help to straighten him out. This man was different from the other farmers; he used me like a human being. It was the best place I had had since coming to Canada.

I found out one thing during this time: the few farmers in the neighbourhood who smoked or drank a little, maybe had the odd game of poker, who were considered the black sheep of the community—they were the people who were nicest to me. I stayed at this place for a year and then worked on my own for a while. By then I realized that there was no future for me in being a hired boy, and made plans to move into Oshawa. In August 1921 I began at General Motors. I worked there for over 44 years.

I am now retired and have a small but comfortable home. When I look back I wonder what I might have been if I had had a normal childhood. Actually I ceased to be a child at the age of 10. No one can understand my feelings of loneliness and despair unless they have lived through it. I think this early life affected me in two ways. My formative years, when I was made to think I was inferior, left me without any confidence in myself. I know there were times when I might have applied for a better position. I felt I could do the job but I just could not push myself forward. I had no faith in myself.

I have also been wary of people who are ardent churchgoers. I know this is unfair to many good people, but I think that if you had been raised amidst a lot of tight-laced Methodists and had the same treatment, you would think I had some cause for this feeling. I would also like to say that years ago Home boys were considered to be bad boys—like boys who had been in a reformatory. This was not the case. They were mostly good boys who were orphaned, or whose parents would, or could, not face up to their responsibilities. Supposing I had not been placed in a Home. What would have become of me?

William Tonkin
Oshawa, Ontario

I got the impression that Canadians had no children of their own and depended on us children.

My brother was 11 years and myself 13 when we left the Liverpool Sheltering Home in February 1909. We sailed on the Corsican and arrived in Halifax one week later. We ended our journey at Knowlton, Quebec. My brother was sent first to a farmer in Cambria, and then to a Mr Campbell in Laguerre, near Huntingdon, Quebec.

I went to live with a farmer by the name of Thomas Wood in Cambria where I stayed for eight years. My boss used to hire French boys from college who could read English but were not good in conversing, so I had a good chance to learn French.

After leaving the farm I worked at the Hotel Victoria. One day my boss, who also ran a livery stable, told me to pick up an inspector for the Bell Telephone Company in St Jerome. Hearing his strong French accent I spoke in French. But to my surprise I learned he was not French.

'You know this country very good' he said to me.

'I should. I've lived here long enough.'

'You born here?'

'No' I said. 'I was born in England.'

'The same place to me. I come from the Mans-ches-ter. My name is Chimey.'

I thought he was kidding but my boss told me it was true. His name was Jimmy O'Brien, and when he was 11 years old he was placed with a French family in Three Rivers. He stayed there for 11 years and did not hear any English spoken.

Some children were lucky and many were respected and showed respect in return. Only one thing they resented. Everybody called them 'Home' boys or 'Home' girls. I got the impression that Canadians had no children of their own and depended on us children. I must have been told this as a joke, but it became fixed in my mind for a while.

Richard Maguire
Montreal, Quebec

At the end of two years my mother came out to Toronto and took me to live with her.

When I had a trip back to Dublin in May 1968, I visited the Smyly Home on Grand Canal Street and the old sweet shop where I spent the few pennies I was lucky to have as a child. The lady in the shop told me that one of the Misses Smyly still visited her shop quite often. She was then over 80 years of age.

My mother placed me in one of the Smyly Homes at three years of age. My father had died and mother was expecting another baby. The Homes accepted children free if the parents could not pay but they expected them to pay if they could. I believe there were three Homes run by the Smylys in Dublin in 1895. They were under the patronage of the British Protestant Society, but I believe the schools accepted all needy children.

I was in the Home until May 1909, when they told my mother that they would send me to Canada or Australia if she paid the fare. I chose Canada and landed at the Coombe Home at Hespeler, Ontario, about the end of May. The master of the Home, a William Tebbs, arranged for me to go to a farm near Branchton. I was about 14 years old—average size, and well built. I was treated fairly well, but I was expected to do a full day's work six days a week. At harvest time the farmers accepted me as a full hired man in exchange for help at threshing time. I was not quite heavy enough to handle the walking plough so the farmer bought a new, single-furrow plough with a seat for riding; these had just come out about this time. He soon taught me to strike out a field, but he had to finish it, as it was too heavy for me to handle.

At the end of two years my mother came out to Toronto with my brother and took me to live with her. The farmer told me he had sent $60 of my wages to the Home. I have never received that money, although I never did apply for it. I have no complaints except that I was left with an inferiority complex about being brought up in an orphanage.

George McDonald
Hamilton, Ontario

I was given 25 cents a day for myself out of my $2.00.

My parents died a few months apart in 1907. I was the middle one of seven children. We were left destitute. The oldest, age 16, went to the British Merchant Marine and my three sisters were raised by relatives. My two brothers and myself were taken in by the Dr Barnardo Homes. I was again the middle one: our ages were 6, 8, and 13. I have memories of Albert Hall on Barnardo day which, I believe, was an annual affair—of royalty there, and a large circular building with a wedge-shaped section filled with Barnardo boys and girls demonstrating their training: naval cadets, gymnastic teams, choral and instrumental groups. In March 1909 we sailed in a party of 100 or more on the Scotian for Portland, Maine. From there we travelled by train to Toronto. After a very short stay in the Toronto Home we went to three separate families in the Niagara Peninsula just a few miles apart.

My main difficulty was having been placed with a young couple in their early twenties. They had a baby five months old. I do not recall any particular affection from them, only an understanding. I addressed them as Mr and Mrs, later by their first names. At social gatherings I was 'our boy from the Barnardo Homes.'

This young couple had settled on a 50-acre farm a year or two earlier. They had built a new house and barn, and were very much dependent on their relatives for their support. I did house and farm chores, walked a mile to a one-room schoolhouse where I received a grammar school education to the age of 14. I was proud that I could handle a team of horses, and plough a straight furrow at age 13. The Home's representative visited about twice each year—usually unexpected. I was encouraged to write regularly to the branch office in Toronto which I did not do.

I recall only one very unpleasant occasion. A gas company was laying a pipe line on the main road in front of the farm. They needed help to dig the ditch for the pipes. My foster father took me with him to help. We worked long hours at $2.00 a day for two weeks. I was given 25 cents a day out of my $2.00 for myself. Knowing that working off the farm was not in accordance with the agreement with the Homes, I told my elder brother about it, and unknown to me he reported it to Toronto.

I do not know what correspondence my foster parents had with the Homes. I did receive a letter from Toronto which was very critical of them, and seemed mostly intended for them to read, which they did. It offered to remove me from their care. They were very upset about this because they did not want me to leave. I replied to the letter, and requested that they allow me to remain there. I stayed until my time was up, which was during my 16th year.

I did not know until my adult life that my foster parents were being paid for my care. I always thought that I was earning my way several times over. During their lifetime I enjoyed close contact with them, and have continued the association with their son and his family—and correspond with them almost on a fortnightly basis. They have been generous and kind, and seem to feel they owe me something.

Upon leaving the farm, I was paid $120 which was by agreement with the Home. I worked a year or so with woodworking machinery in a farm implement factory—joined the Canadian army at 18, and served in France. Finally I went to the United States where I was employed for 27 years by a national organization, in which I progressed to New England district manager, then to self-employment and retirement.

Walter Baker
Milton, Massachusetts

I had to ride the horses' backs to keep from freezing to death.

At the Barnardo Home in London they told us we could join the British Navy or go to Canada. So in 1909 it was Canada for me. There were quite a few Barnardo boys on the ship and we all went to Toronto, stayed a few days and then were sent to different farms in Ontario. I was sent to a farmer at Muirkirk between St Thomas and Windsor.

When I got off the train at Muirkirk there was nobody there to meet me. I walked down the track about a mile. I had no papers to show who I was. Somebody took me back to where I was supposed to go. Right away the farmer gave me a wheelbarrow to get my trunk a mile from the station. Then he sent me to a large field to get the milking cows. It was one of those rail fences with no gates. To get out you were supposed to let the fence down. I walked around that fence for ages before someone came to show me. I was down to Muirkirk in 1966 and the same fence is still there.

The farmer was very strict. I worked from daylight to dark. I was supposed to go to school every winter. No. Never sent to school, or to church or Sunday school. Never went any place. I don't remember how many years I was at the farm. I received a silver medal from the Barnardo Home for being a good boy.

I had one good friend—the farmer next door. He was from the McDonald Home in Scotland. I went to work for him and it was just like home. I stayed at that farm on and off for a year or so. Worked on the railway section for a few months. Then went to Chatham close to Windsor, painting buggies for the Robert Miller buggy works. From there I came back to my farmer friend. His name was Art McConnell.

I left Muirkirk for good when Art asked me if I would like a job looking after a carload of horses that were being shipped to the West from Bothwell, Ontario. That was a tough job in the middle of winter. I had to ride the horses' backs to keep from freezing to death. There were quite a few carloads of horses on the same train. The crew would not give us workers a coach to sit in or sleep in. I made out O.K. Delivered the horses to the right farm. In those days cars and cars of horses were being shipped out West. They had no tractors.

I stayed in the West for the harvest that summer. Then I hit for the North. Stayed in Prince Albert, Saskatchewan, for one winter. Left there and came to The Pas. This was all before World War I. There was hardly any farming here then—it was mostly lumbering, trapping, fishing and mining. I did all those jobs except trapping.

When I came to The Pas there were few white people around. The population was Indians and mixed-bloods. When the war started we didn't hear much about it. We were 200 miles from a post office. In winter we fished and in summer we cut roads so we could haul freight to the Hudson's Bay Company and Revillon Fréres posts farther north. I came down from the North in the spring of 1916, and joined the 200th Battalion. Our Commanding Officer was Judge Bonnycastle. We trained at Camp Hughes. The 199th Battalion from Montreal was short of men so I transferred to Montreal. I went overseas in 1916, was wounded in France April 7, 1918, and came back to Canada before the war was over.

I visited my old friends the McConnells and then went back to The Pas to hunt and fish and haul freight. I got a steady job, married, and worked for Transport Ltd for 37 years until I retired.

I think I did a good thing coming to Canada. Better than staying in England.

Percy White
The Pas, Manitoba

No man could afford to marry me. I'm too expensive to keep.

My life has not been the life of an average Barnardo girl, as I lost both feet through gangrene in January 1910.

When I came to Canada in July 1909 I was in the awkward stage of placing, too old to be boarded, and not old enough for a hired girl, so the arrangement was that I would work for room and board. I was sent to a farm north of Peterborough to a young couple with three small children. Owing to the fact that I had always suffered with chilblains my feet could not stand the intense cold, so gangrene set in. The family was not to blame, as I had made no complaint. The doctor who was called in when I did tell them, took me to Toronto where both feet were amputated. Through the morning paper a collection was taken and artificial feet were bought for me.

I returned to Hazel Brae for five years where I learned to sew. When the Home was given up, there was talk of sending me back to England. I'm glad they didn't, as I have managed pretty well, minding children and sewing. The Canadian government has been very good to me.

I still look after myself. I take a wheelchair for groceries, but I walk and the groceries get the ride. My neighbours are wonderful to me, so I'm a very happy old maid. No man could afford to marry me. I'm too expensive to keep.

I was in Ilford Village Home, Essex, for a few weeks, but was boarded out for five years in Cambridgeshire. My foster dad was in a wheelchair, and his daughter, Rosie Chenery, was born with a deformed back, but a more wonderful man and woman could not be found. I will never forget them.

Anna Hollamby
Toronto

(Anna says she had suffered, from the age of four, a circulation condition called Reynaud's disease. Apparently no information on this condition was given to her foster parents... Ed.)

This course was a Godsend to me and helped me to secure reasonably good jobs.

To start with there were five children in our family, two boys and three girls. My father had quite a nice little business in Derby, England, at the turn of the century, and we lived on the premises. After my youngest sister was born in 1905 our mother contracted pneumonia and passed away, leaving my father with five small children on his hands and a business to tend to. I was really too young to be able to comprehend all the circumstances involved, but it would seem that my father remarried in an effort to keep the family together. From what I learned years later, he made an unwise choice, marrying a widow with three children of her own. This gave her eight to look after. I have never been able to get a clear picture of later events, but it does appear that there was evidence of child neglect insofar as we Webb children were concerned.

The final result was that, through an uncle, my brother and I were taken by Dr Barnardo and sent to the home in London, and subsequently we were sent to Canada. The remaining three girls were taken by aunts and uncles in England.

I was the second eldest, having been born on November 18, 1900. My brother was born in January 1902. As far as I can recall we arrived in Ontario in the spring of 1909, and my brother Albert Edward (Ted) was placed on a small farm a short distance from where I was located. Soon after we were placed, my foster parents sold their farm and moved to Alberta. I was just nine and my brother was seven when we moved away. I never saw him again until many years later in 1921, but we always kept in touch with one another.

Unfortunately, his foster parents mistreated him and kept him out of school on many occasions to do chores on the farm. As for myself, I was more fortunate. I was loved and I had a reasonably happy boyhood in Alberta. When the war broke out in 1914 I had completed my grade eight and was working in a general store. In the spring of 1916 I managed to enlist as a bugler in the 138th Edmonton Battalion. I went overseas in September and remained in England until the spring of 1917.

By this time I was a young man, thinking of my future. The small town where I had grown up was a farming community and opportunities were limited. I stayed at my old job in the general store until 1919 when I was chosen by the Edmonton branch of the Soldiers' Civil Re-establishment to take a course at business college. During the course I was paid $60 a month and my tuition fees were paid. I worked after school and on weekends to clothe myself. This course was a Godsend to me and helped me to secure reasonably good jobs.

In 1933 I married an old school friend from my college days in Edmonton. We had our problems during the Depression years as did many thousands of others, but we raised a lovely family of children—four boys and two girls.

I am now approaching 70 and over the hill as they say. Only one thing I am certain of—my background of life has given me a very insecure and restless nature. As I grew older there was always that question in my mind 'Why, for what reason, did our family have to be broken up?'

Clinton Webb, Sr.
Vancouver, British Columbia

SIX

THE YEAR
1910

I knew then that all I had to do was play the game and do my best and I would have a good home.

By the time I was 12 I could not see any future in England so I worked on my mother until she finally consented to let me leave. About this time—1910—Canada was getting a big boost. All you heard about was this wonderful land of untold opportunities—this land flowing with milk and honey. I decided it was the place for me.

In my case my dad had died when I was three years old, leaving my mother with four children. My three sisters were older, but the eldest was only about 10 so we didn't have it easy. I learned to take care of myself with the toughest, growing up in Birmingham.

Before I sailed for Canada I went into the Middlemore Home for about three months. Life there was good. We were up at seven, washed, brushed our clothes, and shined our shoes. Breakfast was at eight and school at nine. The rules were strict and had to be obeyed. In the group photo I have I count 72 boys, ranging from 7 to 17. With a crowd like that, there had to be discipline.

We left England the last week of May on the Mongolian. My cabin was in steerage; six wood bunks to a cabin, each bunk with a straw mattress and a grey blanket. The cabin was over the works of the ship and the clank of the steering gear together with the whine of the propeller shaft, the smell of hot oil and steam, and no ventilation, drove me out. I spent my nights hidden in a corner on deck against a ventilator shaft for warmth.

On my 12th birthday, June 4th, there was a burial at sea. One of the crew had died. They wrapped him in sail cloth, laid him on a board by the port rail, and stopped the engines. We boys were grouped on deck and sang a hymn and recited the 21st psalm. The captain read the burial service and when he came to 'Earth to Earth', two members of the crew raised one end of the board and slid the body overside. We recited the Lord's prayer and sang another hymn. The engines were started and we were on our way again. I still don't get that 'Earth to Earth' in the middle of the wide Atlantic.

Our first port of call was St John's, Newfoundland, to unload freight. While there we were taken for a walk through the city and up Signal Hill to where Marconi had sent his first trans-Atlantic wireless message. Our destination, Saint John, New Brunswick, was reached two days later.

There had been so much excitement for us youngsters through the trip that none of us had given much thought to the future, but when we landed at Saint John and were divided into two parties, then I think we all realized that we were past the point of no return. We were stepping into the unknown, and there were sinking feelings and tears when we sang 'God be with you till we meet again.'

One party went up towards Moncton and the North Shore. My group went up the Saint John River line. There were heavy hearts as we said good-bye to one after another as they were put off at different stops. Finally at noon, on June 9, 1910, I stepped off the train at Hartland and met my foster father, C.E. Barnett. I will always remember the day. It was one of those rare ones—warm sun, no wind, and the air so clear and quiet you could hear the people greeting each other across the street.

I remember we looked at each other for a long time, he wondering what he had pulled out of the hat; me, starting mental plans on what I was going to do if things got too rough. We went to his mother's for dinner, then back uptown as he had some business to take care of. He told me I could look the town over but to be back where the team was in half an hour. I wasn't interested in the town at that time. I wanted to be by myself and think things out so I walked out on the bridge. It happened that the stream drive was in progress and there were men and teams on both sides of the river rolling logs that had been left high and dry when the water level dropped. Other men were breaking a log jam on a sand bar and moving logs off the bridge piers. I got so interested that I forgot time until I saw Mr Barnett coming out onto the bridge.

'Now then' I thought. 'I've made a good start.'

And I prepared myself for a bawling out. Instead he took the trouble to explain what it was all about and that settled my mind. I knew then that all I had to do was play the game and do my best and I would have a good home.

We loaded the wagon and headed for home, eight miles out back through the woods to a settlement called Pole Hill. There were seven families there altogether. I met my foster mother. She was a grand person too, but it took a long time to really know her. They had no children of their own so I expect it was hard for them to get used to a boy around the place. Now, looking back over the years I can see she loved her boy very much, but just did not know how to show it without seeming soft. Perhaps a lot of it was my fault. I had been brought up in a world where you had to fight your way and show no quarter or sink.

But there were many times when an arm around her boy and a bit of sympathy would have helped over the rough spots. One incident has stayed with me. It is laughable now, but at the time it was big. It was my first Christmas. I received presents—for the very first time in my life and I was 12 years old. I got an orange, a mouth organ and a thin book—Tiny Tim by Charles Dickens.

We went to Grandma Barnett's for dinner and when we got back home we found the pup had chewed Tiny Tim to shreds and had ruined the mouth organ. I loved music and had planned to master it. Being a boy, I could not cry, but the pup dropped considerable in my estimation. The worst hurt was Ma. She said the pup had enjoyed his Christmas too. An arm around her boy and a few right words would have made a world of difference.

I guess I settled in without trouble. I liked to work and of course it was all new which made it more interesting. I learned to swing a flail without hitting my ear and thresh beans on the barn floor and then finally to pick them over on the kitchen table in the evening. It was real pioneer life. My socks, mitts, and even underwear were hand-knit from wool carded and spun from our own sheep. A winter evening chore was to help spin and hank the yarn. And did you ever make a pair of shoepacs? Here's how. Get the hide from the two hind legs of a small deer, measure the length you want for your foot from the hock towards the hoof, cut and sew them up with rawhide and cut the length of leg you want and there you have it. These shoepacs, worn hair-side in, are the warmest things you can have on your feet. And if you turn them hair-side out you have the best no-skid footwear you could find. Fine if you're booming logs out on the river or lake ice and the logs are coming at you and you have to move fast.

We had a school there—a single room with a stove in the middle. I went for part of two terms. There was too much work to do and it was too cold to go in winter. I got my schooling by correspondence in later years.

Evenings were short. We would be in bed by nine or soon after, as six in the morning seemed to come all too soon. Like most we subscribed to the popular Family Herald and Weekly Star and read it by the light of the coal-oil lamp. There was no telephone, no electricity, no indoor plumbing. We carried drinking water from the spring and made our own soap. In spring we tapped the maple trees for syrup and sugar. I seldom went to town. There was no money, so why bother? In summer I got my pleasure from fishing in the brook that ran through the farm. When we were low on meat someone would be delegated to shoot a deer and divide it up among all the families.

I enlisted on my 18th birthday in 1916—not for any patriotic reason, but to get rid of a brown suit that I hated. The old folks had bought it for three dollars plus a night's lodging, from an Armenian peddlar who tramped through the country with a pack on his back. Three dollars was such a lot of money that I hated to let the folks think they had wasted it.

While I was in France they sold the farm and bought another across the river from Hartland. I expect they thought their boy would settle down after the war, but farming was not for me. I followed the electrical trade and retired as district superintendent of a large corner of Saskatchewan. So it has been a full life.

Jim Eccleston
Regina, Saskatchewan

They were real parents to me.

My life in Birmingham, England, was anything but pleasant. I lived with a lady who didn't have much money, so she would get hooks and eyes and cards from a factory and I helped to sew them on the cards for food and a few things to wear. This is what I was doing when Miss Frances Kirby found me. She took 'me away from there and put me into a convalescent home for two weeks, as I was in very poor health. Then she got me into a private home in Liverpool run by an elderly lady, Miss Hornby, who was connected with the Liverpool Sheltering Homes.

I was only eight years old and had never had a chance to go to school, so it was quite a thing for me to go to school and be with other children. Miss Hornby taught me to read, which I couldn't do when I went there. I still have the book that she taught me to read from. I went to school for about two years before coming to Canada in 1910. Miss Hornby made arrangements to send me and another girl by the name of Amy Banks who was much older. Amy was to look after me on the boat.

We left Liverpool on May 19, 1910, on the Corsican, arrived in Quebec, and then onto the train for the Knowlton Home in Quebec. I was there around two weeks when I was taken by Mr and Mrs John Wallace of Kingsbury. They were real parents to me and I was very happy. They thought as much of me as they did of their own. I went to school until I was 16.

Then I stayed at home to help my mom as she wasn't always too well. She passed away in May 1919, and I stayed with dad until I was married in 1923 to a veteran of World War I. My dad stayed with me until he died in 1933 at the age of 80. I thought as much of them as if they had been my own flesh and blood.

I really have a lot to thank Miss Kirby for, because I don't think that I would be here today if she hadn't found me in Birmingham. She was the one who changed my whole pattern of life.

I do not know anything about my parents. I have never been back to England, and I have never had any desire to go.

Mary Wallace Blake
Née Woodhall
Kingsbury, Quebec

My goodness but it's awful quiet in this country.

One day at school I was called out of the room by my teacher, Miss Annie Fenton, and a very portly, well-dressed man with a very large gold chain across his rounded torso was patting me on the head and asking questions. 'How do you like school?' he wanted to know. He followed this by other remarks as to my mother being widowed with the burden of having five girls and two boys to support. How would I like to go to a large Home with other boys and eventually learn a trade, or music, or seafaring? Or would I like to try a colonial life in Australia or Canada with an older sister to keep me company on the journey? I loved domestic animals and the thought of a big new country. I figured that I couldn't go wrong.

I was nine years old then and I had only a hazy idea of Canada. But like all boys of that age my mind was on fire. In 1909 the standard of living was very poor in the coal-mining town where I lived. I played in an open space at the back of the coal miners' homes. To go to the park or anywhere that had trees and grass and plants was an exciting experience. The idea of wide open spaces and cowboys and Indians inflamed my imagination.

At home my mother was giving me the story of how boys had to leave the nest sooner or later and telling her boy the same things that all mothers tell their offspring who are about to leave the old place. So eventually I found myself in the Barnardo Home at Epsom, England. The following spring, in 1910, I was told that I would be going to Canada with a group of picked boys and with other children from the Homes in London, including my older sister.

We sailed in March, 1910, on the Sicilian. During the voyage my mind was devoid of thoughts of the future. I was having a lot of fun playing games on deck with boys and girls of the same age. We had a different sense of freedom and plenty of good food and fresh air which kept the bloom on our cheeks.

We docked at Portland, Maine, and my first impression of North America was so disappointing. I well remember the dismal scene—dirty snow, bare and leafless trees, sullen dark clouds, and sad, dirty, lifeless, brown fields and grass. I wondered what the interior of the country would be like—not realizing that this was always a drab time—at the end of winter.

From Maine we took a train to Toronto and after three or four days of rest at the Jarvis Street Home, I was called in and given instructions for travel to my foster home. The conductor of the train (it was the Mariposa Grand Trunk Railway) was to see that I got off at the right station.

I dismounted when I was told to and stood on the platform feeling like a lost sheep. I was the only one on that platform, but through the window I saw a middle-aged lady who seemed to be watching my every movement and giving me a very thorough eye-gazing. I later learned that she was to be my foster mother, as it was her son—a farmer—who was to meet me. She was taking a trip on that day to visit relatives in a nearby town.

Soon a very large man of heavy proportions walked up to me and with kind of a silly grin on his face asked me if I was looking for someone. I said I was looking for a Mr Chester Archer, and he said he guessed he was the man.

'Well, Johnny, come along' he said. 'I will call you Johnny because I like that better than John.' (He should have known that my nickname at Wallsend was Fatty Atkinson.)

Well, in 1910, travel was by horse or 'shanks mare' so I had a horse and buggy ride for three miles along farm fields with a man who did not say 10 words at a time. But he sure was listening to my gabbing. I remember stopping my talk and him asking me what I was thinking about. I said 'My goodness, but it's awful quiet in this country.' He gave a big laugh. I think my brogue tickled him somehow. He was a good man. He never said much, but he could grin like a Cheshire cat on occasion.

I soon adapted to farm life, my new neighbours, and going to the village church. I went to school for six winters, to all the grades they had. My school marks and my ability to sing at public functions and in church made my foster family proud of me.

When my five-year agreement was up in April 1916 I was free to make my own decisions. The Great War was on. Three Barnardo boys in the area had already gone into the army and I decided to enlist too. I was sent to England and one day in Epsom, when I was in a Canadian Base Hospital there, I decided to walk downtown with a French-Canadian chum and we got talking to two girls. I told my friend that I wanted the girl with the dark hair and the dark fur on her shoulders—and sure enough that girl became my wife after the war when I got out of Germany and back to London.

I returned to Canada, and my wife joined me two months later. Unfortunately I took sick—an aftermath of the war and other things—and had to spend a winter in the Veterans' Hospital at Kingston, Ontario. When I got feeling better my wife and I decided to visit my sister who had come out from England at the same time I had. She had married a Cleveland boy, so we visited them there—and have lived in Cleveland ever since—51 years.

I call my foster family in Canada every Christmas Eve. Chester Archer is dead now, but his wife is still living in a nursing home in Little Britain, Ontario. He married while I was overseas and they had a son who later took over the farm and is now a grandpa with boys of his own.

So we have lived through a transition from the horse and buggy days and the first telephones and street cars and the first hand-operated gramophones and hand-cranked Fords to the fast crazy world of today. As the fellow said, 'It's enough to jar your mother's preserves.'

John H. Atkinson
Cleveland, Ohio

What did you want to get such a small child for?

I did not want to come over but my brother Jim was older and he wanted to come. I kept saying that I wanted to go home to my mother, but I knew she was ill with a bad heart and father—he had lung trouble—so we did not have much to say about it. We sailed for Canada in March 1910 when I was 10 years old.

I was only at the Home in Knowlton, Quebec, for one day when a maiden lady, Miss Sarah Jane Williams, came up from Sweetsburg to pick out a girl. There were 12 of us in line like stairs. I was the shortest and the oldest one and she picked me. My clothes were not ready so I was not able to go home with Miss Williams. Her brother came after me the following Monday.

I was broken-hearted at leaving my brother, but Miss Louisa Birt said she would try to get him in a home near me, which she did.

Miss Williams' mother was alive when I went there. She was blind and she had to feel me all over. She said 'What did you want to get such a small child for?' Of course that hurt me. But 'Mother Williams' got so she loved me and she was always 'mother' to me.

Mother had a stroke in March 1915, and passed away in January 1917, at the age of 89 years and two days. She was in bed all that time and I fed her three times a day.

I lived at home with Miss Williams, until I married on December 21, 1929. After that I used to go home once a week. Miss Williams was very ill in 1933. I went home to take care of her. Then again in 1934 she was ill from May 18 to September 30. I stayed with her all the time. I could not seem to leave her. And what hurts me most was that she never knew me. My husband, she knew him every time she saw him. After a while the doctor told me I had to go for a walk every day or I would not be able to carry on.

Some time after Miss Williams passed away I had a letter from Miss Birt saying she was coming to Knowlton. She wanted me and my husband to go to see her. She said she would let me know when she would be there and when to come. So we went up to see her. We wrote a few times after that but she was not young and she must have passed away after that last visit or she would have continued to write.

I do not remember England too well, but I did write to my father and mother and brothers over the years. One brother was killed in World War I. The other two brothers came through the war. In 1918 I had one young brother left in England and Mr Williams sent him a boat ticket to come to Canada. He was 13 years old when he arrived in March. There were nine children in our family eight boys and me—the only girl. There is just my brother Jim and me left.

I will close by saying that I never repaid Miss Williams for what she did for me. I did all I could for her. When she was ill for the first time her brother wanted the doctor to put her in the hospital. She said 'No, I have Mary and that is all I want.' (She did not like my name Pollie so she asked

Miss Birt if she could call me Mary). The doctor said that she was getting better care than if she was in the hospital. When she passed away and her will was read, she left everything to me. Even the first cent she earned, I guess.

I am one in a good many Home children who can say they had a real good home. None better.

Mrs Pollie Jones
West Brome, Quebec

Each place we would go the wives would ask us how Mrs So-and-So served out the food... the women would all try to outdo each other.

Just after Christmas, 1910, I went down to the Salvation Army in Edinburgh, Scotland, and booked passage to Canada for myself and a friend called Fletcher Welch. We packed our kit bags and took the train to Glasgow. Here the Sicilian awaited us. Seemingly this ship had just unloaded a cargo of cattle and was now returning to Canada. The deck had been flushed down with hoses, then bunks were built—six people to each section. So, hi-ho, we were off to the land of promise—of cowboys, Indians and wide open spaces. I was 20 years old.

What a trip. The first stop was to pick up mail, which was brought to us in a small boat near the tip of Ireland. Then we were out in the sea, heading straight for Halifax. Thirteen and a half days of sea-tossing, with the decks all roped for passenger safety. I bet the propeller was out of the water half the time. This shook the ship something awful. First we would seem to be reaching for the skies; next reaching for the bottom of the ocean. As a change of pace, we would roll from side to side. The ship was covered with ice a foot or two deep on every chain and rope. Mother, why did I ever leave home?

On the whole trip I was only seasick once. I went into the smoking lounge and—being a non-smoker—that upset my stomach. I should add that during the trip, food was the farthest thing from our minds. Wooden tables had been set up in the middle of the floor. Then it was come and get it. The place stank of greasy cooking; the smell took all thoughts of eating away. I guess most of us lived on fresh air. No kidding.

We had a pot-bellied stove for heating—burned soft coal—and beside the stove was a large apple barrel to hold the coal. I remember the barrel well, because of an incident. My chum Fletcher was real seasick and confined to his bunk for days. One of the young men suggested we get Fletcher up to go for a walk. Fletcher got as far as the stove, reached for the apple barrel and sat on it. Suddenly the boat took a savage heave to one side. Away went Fletcher on the open-top barrel—bang to the side of the wooden partition. Then the ship changed her mind and lurched to the other side. The barrel hit the wall with a hefty wallop. This jack-knifed Fletcher firmly into it and believe me when I say it took some yanking to get him out. He returned to his bed and stayed there for the rest of the journey.

The Sicilian landed in Halifax in typically beautiful Canadian weather—very cold. I was wearing a two-piece flannel suit, kid boots, no hat or gloves and no underwear. I was lucky in a way, because some of the chaps aboard were going back to the silver mines in Cobalt. I said to them 'What do you have to wear in this cold?' They took me in tow and off we went to the second-hand stores. It was quite a transformation. I wondered what my mother would have thought if she had seen me. Her last words to me on leaving home were 'Now you've got a good Scotch tongue in your head—use it.' This took away most of my shyness.

The Salvation Army in Toronto got me a job on a farm near Draycott, outside of Guelph, Ontario. Next thing I knew I was on one end of a cross-cut saw. Then we tapped the maple trees for their sap. Stayed two months. I got a letter from my pal saying that on the farm next to him a hired man was wanted. I went out and accepted the job. This farm was about nine miles outside of Brantford, Ontario. It wasn't a place where you would get rich because the salary was $10 per month. A week consisted of seven days—5.00 a.m. till 8.00 p.m. I suppose the farmer thought that busy hands kept a person out of mischief.

The hired girl was a Barnardo Home girl. Her brother from the same Home worked some place near us. In this area the farmers used to send their hired hands to other farmers to help in harvesting the crops. Each place we would go to, the wives would ask us how Mrs So-and-So served out the food. We would say this and that was on the table—and make it good. Then the women would all try to outdo each other.

In the spring of 1911, I hired out to a farmer who did mixed farming. I had to milk my share of the cows—curry horses—clean out the barn—breakfast—and be out in the field at 6.00 a.m. This farmer was pleased with me. He told me after a year's work that I had done more work than his previous hired man had done in three years, and he offered me his hundred-acre farm with no down payment. Said in three years it would pay for itself. I left in the spring of 1912 because I was afraid. Me, being born in the city, take on the job of running a farm? The house was a two-storey brick building and there was a beautiful large barn, half stone and half wood, the cow and horse part all cemented. Do you think me a coward?

My next move was to Carberry, Manitoba. Worked for G. B. Murphy & Sons at the Pine Creek Ranch—horses and cattle—stayed 19 months—wages, $40 per month. From there I was all over the country—ploughing, seeding. Worked lots around Regina and Saskatoon. After seeding was over I worked on government grading outfits, putting in culverts in low places.

Harvesters' wages were $1.75 a day—6.00 a.m. till 6.00 p.m. Up in Lang, Saskatchewan we got $1.75 per day to start but the fellow who owned the threshing machine raised our daily pay to $2.00 —said it was the best gang he ever had and did not want to lose us so gave us the extra two bits. I worked in the bush in Emo, Ontario, for seven months. You name it and I'm sure I've done it. My life has been one round of pleasure. I was considered a good worker. At least I was never afraid of it.

In the midst of my wanderings I spent five years in France and Belgium during World War I. Was even good enough to leave some of my blood. I left Cambrai in France in 1919, after almost a full five years in the army. Then I came back to Toronto for a few weeks. Meals were 25 cents for soup, meat and potatoes, pie, tea or coffee. Costs that for a cup of coffee now. Times have changed.

Hugh West
Winnipeg, Manitoba

I never heard of anyone I belonged to.

It may have been my mother who used to visit me in the orphanage, because when we were getting on the boat, she had me by the arm and she took the earrings out of my ears. I don't remember too much of England. I was in the Annie Macpherson Home there until a Reverend Mr Parks took me away. I never heard of anyone I belonged to. I've cried many a night because I had no one to call my mother, and I have always said I never would want to see England again, for I have no sweet memories of anything or anyone.

I was in Canada a few years before World War I. My maiden name was Mary Alice Doncaster. I was told that my family in England lived on Seven Sisters Road, but I don't know if that is true or not. I must have been about eight years old when I came to Canada. Now I am in my 60s. I have seven nice children all married, except one son.

Surely in England, I must have someone.

Mary Alice Wunder, née Doncaster
Kitchener, Ontario
(There is a Seven Sisters Road in north London, England. Ed.)

When the pigs become satisfied with the peas, it is a job to keep them from roving.

The Fegan Home in Stony Stratford, Buckinghamshire, had a lovely rural atmosphere. There were 140 boys there. We had our own school, chapel, dining hall, gymnasium and three dormitories, also a large playground and adjacent cricket and football field. Our weekday dress was jersey, knickers, stockings, cap, and boots. The Sabbath saw us in grey Norfolk jackets, deep Eton-type collars, and bow ties.

I had been placed in 'Stony' in 1906 when I was seven years of age. My mother had died the previous year and our home at Bromley-by-Bow had been vacated. I had no sisters, and Hector, my only brother, went to live with relatives on my mother's side. Father made a home with kinfolk of his own.

Piety at Fegan's was a major precept. We attended chapel twice on Sunday, had prayer and scripture reading morning and evening in the dining hall, and sang Grace before and after each meal. Meals followed a fairly close pattern:

On Monday we have soup
On Tuesday we have rice
On Wednesday we have treacle tart
And that is very nice
On Thursday we have beefsteak
On Friday we have fish
On Saturday we have roly-duff
And that is all we wish.

Sunday and its menu seems to have escaped this weekly round-up, yet Sunday's food, if anything, was a bit superior in quantity and quality to that of the rest of the week.

Naturally, living together like this nurtured an affinity and an affection among groups of lads. We studied together in school and performed certain allotted duties about the kitchens, dining hall, dormitories, and grounds. 'It is understandable that, when in April there would be the so-called 'hiving-off' of boys deemed fit for emigration to Canada, genuine sorrow would be felt by some destined to go. I well recall the heartbreak of the farewell gatherings for the 'Canadians' as the chosen emigrants were called.

In 1910, my turn came. I was a 'Canadian'. The period prior to leaving England seemed to be characterized by a little more leniency in discipline towards those who were leaving. Our short-cropped hair was allowed to grow. We were introduced to Canadian coinage, and were taught something of Canadian geography and history. I seemed also to sense that the grief at leaving the Home could be tempered by the excitement of anticipation and that anticipation could give way to realization when the first leg of the journey took us to Southwark where there was for each boy a small steamer trunk of his own. It contained a goodly outfit of clothing, a Bible, a Sankey hymnal, a number of books pertaining to the scriptures, and a writing case.

I was 11 years of age in April 1910, and a dear grandmother who came with other relatives to bid me farewell at Southwark said simply 'Colin, you will soon be in your teens.'

Our party embarked from Liverpool on the Canadian Pacific liner Empress of Ireland. The Governor, as Mr Fegan was respectfully called, accompanied us on the voyage and came with us by way of the old colonist train from Halifax to Toronto. The coaches were primitive indeed. One day the train stopped for a lengthy spell at some country point. We were all allowed to get out for a leg stretch and some refreshment. As we left the car, Mr Fegan stood at the outlet with a basin of warm water, some soap, a wash cloth and a towel. Each boy was given a refreshing rub over the hands and face and a kindly word from 'The Governor'. The incident did not carry great significance with me until years later. Then the words 'Inasmuch as ye have done it unto the least of these, my brethren' brought the memory of J.W.C. Fegan indelibly to my mind.

My home, upon arriving in Canada, was with a family on a farmstead at Orono, in Durham County, Ontario. I remained with them from 1910 to 1947. The lady of the house was a daughter of a Methodist parson—a wonderful housewife and manager and a qualified musician. She shared her gift for music for upwards of 40 years as organist and choir director at the local church. They had one child, a son, now a professor at Guelph University. Needless to say my training at Fegan's and my fortunate access to a Christian home here have left me with sympathetic views of the church.

I was married in 1949 and in April 1968 I experienced the sorrow of losing my beloved wife by death. I reached my 70th birthday in August 1969 and a friend commented upon the fact that I had reached the biblical 'three score years and ten'. I was reminded of grandmother Taylor's 'Colin, you will soon be in your teens', and wondered if I would have seen the 70 mark if destiny had not seen fit to bring me to Canada.

Early in 1951, my wife and I visited England. We went with a London friend to Bromley-by-Bow. Knapp Road where I had lived was a shambles from the bombing. The school that I had attended at the age of three was a wreck. The house at number 39 where I was born remained standing, however, throughout the ordeal.

To supplement memory's pictures of those early years in Canada I have one or two prized snapshots taken by a gentleman who would come in the summertime to visit the numerous Fegan boys in the district. On one of these visits he found me minding a group of pigs in a field where there was a great quantity of shelled ripe peas following the harvest. Unlike the father of the Prodigal Son the visitor did not fall upon my neck and kiss me. He merely said 'My boy, how are you getting along?'

I replied 'Splendidly, sir, only when the pigs become satisfied with the peas, it is a job to keep them from roving.'

Is it not so that the roving instinct is common to both those of us who have become satisfied, and those for whom this fortunate state seems the farther removed? Perhaps there is assurance in our hope of the hereafter where eating and drinking are not of primary importance and where, hopefully, the peas will have all been gleaned beforehand.

Colin Taylor
Bowmanville, Ontario

I made up my mind to make the best of it and be a Canadian—even to discarding the English accent.

I can just remember Dr Barnardo. He had a loving pat for all of us little boys, but some of the ding-a-lings working in the Homes weren't so nice.

I was put in the Home when I was four, and spent five lovely years in a farm home not far from Yarmouth. Then, I returned to London in 1910 and one Saturday morning I left with a group of boys to go on board an old Allan Line steamer. We stopped at Le Havre, France to load cargo and more passengers and sailed for Canada on Tuesday afternoon.

From Toronto I was sent to the Muskoka District where I spent two and a half years. It was not too pleasant. In fact it was just the opposite. Then in 1913 I was transferred to a farm near London, and shortly I was transferred again.

I landed here at Harrow, Ontario, in June 1914, and here I've been ever since. I finished my growing up here, raised my family, and while I haven't set the world on fire, I've taken my place in the community and haven't a thing to be ashamed of.

In view of events in this country I've put in application for proof of Canadian citizenship. When I first arrived here I made up my mind to make the best of it and be a Canadian—even to discarding the English accent.

William Houghton
Harrow, Ontario

SEVEN

THE YEARS
1911–1912

He spoke mainly his own language to his wife and relatives...I was sure I would die of loneliness, but little boys don't die so easy.

Being a 'Home Boy' was no bed of roses. I was nine years old when I arrived at Halifax, May 4, 1912, aboard the Corsican. I was under the auspices of the Annie Macpherson Home in London, so my first stop was their distribution centre in Stratford, Ontario. From there I was farmed out to whoever was looking for farm help.

My boss wanted an older boy but he was late by three weeks and there were just a few of us runts left to choose from. I was happy to get away from the Home and into my new adventure. I don't know what I expected. We were conditioned to think great things were in store for us—that Canada was one big apple tree, and our worries were over for life. It wasn't my fault that I picked a wormy apple. That much I knew.

The boss was the son of a European immigrant, married, with one son 18 months old, and 50 acres of land near Mitchell, Ontario. He weighed over 200 pounds, had a heavy accent, and spoke mainly his own language to his wife and relatives. I damn near died of loneliness. For the first time in my life I began to hate my father who, my mother said, was to blame for the family breakup. I was sure I would die, but little boys don't die so easy.

A brother two years older was put in the Annie Macpherson Home with me but he ran away and ended up in the Barnardo Home. He arrived in Canada a month ahead of me, sometime in April, 1912. He was farmed out at Caledon or Caledonia, I forget which—but not too far from Toronto. This put him over 100 miles from me but I began to plan to run away to be near him.

My first winter in Canada was not too bad. I went to school for six months. I was well fed, well clothed and mingling with other children helped a lot. But 'Home Boy' carried a stigma even among kids. I retaliated by getting the highest marks and some of them came to me to get help with arithmetic, which boosted my morale considerably.

Calamity hit me in April 1913 when my mother wrote to tell me that my brother had committed suicide. Now I did not even have a dream to run to. I became surly, lippy, and don't-give-a-damnish until my boss was just about ready to give up on me. He was the toughest so I played a game of submitting and waiting. My only escape was an English family with a son my age and three girls each a year or so older. They had a piano and we had some jolly sing-songs.

Then in 1914 fate played one of those sardonic tricks. England went to war against the Germans the race my boss belonged to—and this bloody little Englishman was not allowed to forget it. At the age of 14 I was 'allowed' to quit school and work full time on the farm for $40 for the year—minus the cost of my clothes and doctor's bills. At this point you may inject every phase of child slave labour you have ever heard of. I was expected to do a man's work, long hours and no recreation whatever. The most outstanding turn of events came just after the 1918 armistice. I suddenly became the white-haired boy.

'Yes, you can have a horse and cutter to drive to the skating rink at Mitchell. Do you have enough money?'

'Yes, you can buy a bicycle in the spring.'

They bent over backwards to be nice, but that could not wipe out the resentment, that had built up in me. I fully intended to leave at the end of my contract year, March 19, 1919, when lightning struck again. They offered me $300 to stay until the harvest was in. This was equivalent to $10 a month more than top wages for a man in those parts. I took it.

In the fall I went to a lumber camp and the next spring to a construction job. There I met a young fellow from Toronto who was interested in boxing. When the job was done we went to Toronto and joined a good athletic club. Every evening for six months we worked out on the light and heavy bags, skipped rope, and sparred in the ring. After that I was no longer the patsy from the sticks but a cause to be respected.

(First name withheld by request) Miller
Vancouver, B.C.

His wife was a bad woman. I could not go anywhere but what she was after me...

Our home was in a little town called Hampton Wick. My father was wounded in the Boer War very bad, and was not able to care for us, which is why my sister Mabel and I were placed in the Dr Barnardo Home. An older brother Robert was placed in a different Home than we were, Quarrier Homes of Scotland, for what reason we never knew. We have never heard from him from that day to this.

My sister and I came to Canada in 1911. She was 13 and I was 11. We landed in Quebec City and from there we were sent to a farm in Pembroke, Ontario, to a married man who had one boy and two girls. They used Mabel and me very badly. If we made a mistake of any kind we were beaten, and we were never allowed to go to school. Three years later this man ran for a civic job in Pembroke and won. Mabel and I were then sent to another farmer by the name of Peter Hamilton. Here we were used better. In the year 1919 my sister got married to a returned man called Archie A. Anderson. They were happily married and are still living together after 51 years of marriage.

My next boss was another farmer, a very nice man who treated me good, but his wife was a bad woman. I could not go anywhere but what she was after me, not for anything I had done, but for me myself. It got so bad that I had to run away from there.

I went to work in the lumber camps where nobody could speak English, just French, but I got along fine. I learned to speak French, also to read and write it. It sure came in handy to me in later years. From the lumber camps I went to work as a fireman for the old Grand Trunk Railway, but misfortune overtook me. I developed heart trouble so I asked for a transfer to build steam locomotives at the Fort Rouge boiler shop in Winnipeg, Manitoba. I stayed at this until I was forced to retire because of my heart.

I am happily married with seven children: two boys and five girls.

Patrick Thomas Markham
Winnipeg, Manitoba

The men were indecent so I left there on my own account.

One thing was lacking in the boarding-out Home in Kent and that was love. My sister Gertrude and I were punished for things that most people would not think of so we ran away. We had been there for eight years—ever since my mother passed away after the birth of my youngest brother.

Then we were taken to the Girls' Village Home in Essex. It was a lovely quiet place. Just inside the gates was a monument of Dr Barnardo. After about two months we were told we would be going to Canada. I can hardly describe how we felt. I had read only a little about Canada in our school books. In one story it was described as a cold country where a man had had his legs frozen. In another story a man and lady in a horse and cutter were chased by wolves.

I remember that we were given all new clothes for the trip. We had blue serge jumpers and blouses and heavy undergarments to wear on board ship. We also had canvas shoes and each one of us had a trunk with good clothing, and a Bible and a book of rules.

I cannot remember the trip from the Girls' Village to Liverpool, but I do remember going on board ship—walking up the gang-plank and going down into the ship. I was 11 years old and my sister had her 13th birthday on board. The ship was the Sicilian and the year was 1912. We were happy on board with the other girls. We played games and we were allowed some money to buy candies. The sailors and the Captain were very good to us.

One morning I woke up with my face half covered with eczema. They called the doctor and he gave the nurse something to put on my face. When we arrived in Halifax in late September we had to pass immigration and on account of my eczema the officers took me to one side and were not going to let me go. My sister started to cry so someone spoke to them and they let me pass.

One thing I remember about the train ride to Peterborough was the hard-boiled eggs that we had with bread and butter. Then at the Home in Peterborough we had syrup on our bread, and cocoa. We thought it was a great treat.

The first people I went to were a Scotch family, a Mr and Mrs James Mitchell. They were good to me, but I did not get along at school. It was too much of a change from the English school. I found the history of Canada and the arithmetic very hard and the teacher was unpleasant. He would not explain the difference in money to me. Later he was expelled.

I stayed just a short time in that home. The next one I went to the lady was pleasant but the men were indecent, so I left there on my own account. The lady was going to leave me there alone to keep house for two weeks. She had left me alone for a week just a while before that and I found the men were indecent. So I told the lady I would write to Peterborough and leave. When she left to visit her sister I got on the train with her. I had my 13th birthday while I was in that place.

From Peterborough I went to Cambray and to a Christian family. Their names were Mr and Mrs Frank Riches and for the first time I knew what it was to be a member of a family who thought something of me. Mrs Riches passed away after her last baby was born and Mr Riches remarried when the baby was 11 months old. He told me that his home was my home but I left shortly after to work for a Mr and Mrs William Newman. They were another wonderful Christian couple and it was from their home that I was married. Later Mr Newman was elected Member of Parliament for Victoria and Haliburton Counties.

The only thing—when I left England it was a bad time to change schools. I did not seem to pick up the school work in Canada but had the teacher been kind and understanding I might have got along.

Mrs Selina M. Barker
Willowdale, Ontario

'No! He's only a Home boy we've got.' It's a wonder he didn't say 'we— call him Fido'.

The air in Canada seemed cold. I noticed the train whistles. I'd never heard them in England. It was March 1911. I was not quite nine years old and I had just got off the Sicilian. After a long train ride I reached the Barnardo Home on Peter Street in Toronto. From there I was sent to a farm near Port Colborne, Ontario. I was met by one of the sons, Bill—24 years old—who drove me to his mother's farm in a horse and cutter. He lived with her and his brother George, age 20. The father had been dead some years. I slept with Bill that night but that was the only time, as I wet the bed. So I was put in an attic room to sleep by myself.

I walked one mile to school daily and did the chores night and morning. I had to gather eggs, feed the chickens, carry in wood and water. Six months later I milked cows, morning and night. Now like other nine-year-old boys I played around when I should have been working. For this I got plenty of the horse whip from George who was a bit of a sadist anyway. After a couple of years I wrote to my mother in England complaining of George's horse-whipping activities on me and she went to the Barnardo Home in Stepney, London. They contacted Toronto and a man was sent to fetch me.

After a few days in Toronto I went to a farmer in central Ontario where I was sent to school until I was 14 years old. In those days any farmer could keep his son out of school permanently as soon as he was 14. I finished eighth grade at 14 and then the farmer loaned me for a year and a half to his married son who had a farm three miles away. He worked me like a slave. When someone would say to him 'Is that your son?' he would say 'No! He's only a Home boy we've got.' It's a wonder he didn't say 'We call him Fido'.

When I was 15 1/2 years old I wrote to the Home in Toronto and said that if they didn't take me away from there I would run away. I was shipped to Toronto and there I was intimidated by a man named Campbell for daring to complain.

A week later I was surprised to be sent back to Port Colborne to the farm right across the road from the first farm. This neighbour had seen me working and wrote to Toronto asking for me. He treated me like one of his family—even took me fishing. I liked him enough to call him Dad and years later I came from Western Canada and visited him.

When I turned 17 I was my own boss—turned loose in the world with $20. I went to North Bay, Ontario, and worked in a sawmill for $2.75 a day, 10 hours a day and I paid $1.00 a day for board at a place half a mile away. When I had enough money I went to Montreal and got a job with the Great North Western telegraph office on St Francis Xavier Street. In August I quit and bought a harvest excursion ticket to Winnipeg for $12. If you wanted to go farther west you paid one cent a mile as far as Calgary and Edmonton. Everybody had to take their own food and blankets.

I left Montreal without enough food to get me to Winnipeg so when we got to Kenora and the train stopped for half an hour I hurried to the stores a short distance away and bought a dozen peaches. Just then the train whistle blew. I didn't stop for my change but ran back to the station in the August heat. The peaches bounced up and down in the paper bag and then, just as I landed on the platform, a hole came in the bag and the peaches fell out. The passengers cheered and laughed and I barely made it onto the train without being killed, as it had picked up so much speed.

I went to Vancouver after the harvest, then to Prince Rupert, on to Alaska, and then back to Vancouver. That's how I saw Canada coast to coast in the 1920s. I worked on road construction, in copper mines, lumber camps and sometimes on farms. Farms were the last resort because of the longer hours for less money. For a while I worked for the Canover brothers who ran the Vancouver Heights Dairy. I delivered milk with a horse in 1924. Then I built a small house in North Burnaby but I didn't spend time in it. I was in logging camps at Orford Bay, at Greenway Sound near Alert Bay, at Oscar Soderman's camp at Viner Sound near Ocean Falls, at Cowichan Lake, Alberni, and the Campbell River Lumber Company. When the Depression arrived in 1933 I was laid off and there were no jobs available after that.

In 1934 about one-third of Burnaby's population was on relief. Single men were cut to 25 cents a day to live on. Later the government took over all unemployed single men and sent them to relief camps three or more miles from any town. They got free work clothes, tobacco and food and $15 a month. The camps were run by the Department of National Defence. The top man was usually a major who used unemployed bosses from closed-down construction projects to handle the men. There were no drills or army uniforms but each man had a number. Men from 15 to 75 years of age cut trails in the forest in the winter and repaired roads in the summer.

I sold my house in Burnaby to pay my debts and had enough money left to buy a ticket to Winnipeg. From there I stole rides on freight trains. Often there were 50 men in one box car. I rode the rods to Montreal, worked my way on a cattle boat to Glasgow, and from there I rode trucks down to London to see my relatives whom I hadn't seen for 25 years. This was the biggest mistake I ever made in my life. After living in Canada I couldn't live in England. My Canadian ideas of social classes weren't acceptable to even my family who were working people.

They decided they had to bring me in line—told me who I should visit and what I should wear. So I took off on my own without any money.

I walked over a lot of England and I sometimes got work at 10 pence an hour. After a year and a half of this I got fed up and joined the English army so I could get out of the country. In 1939 I was shipped to Singapore. Two and a half years later in February 1942 the Japanese took us prisoners of war. I was in various camps in Thailand, nearly always on the river Mekong. I helped to build the railway to Burma. There's an English, Canadian, Dutch, or Australian soldier buried there for nearly every wooden tie supporting the steel rails. If the war had lasted another six months I wouldn't be alive today. The atom bomb saved my life.

I'm 68 years old now. I'm a professional gardener and landscaper, own a late model pick-up truck and my own home. I wouldn't have either one if I'd always lived in England. I wouldn't go back to England if you gave me a free ticket and a life pension.

But looking back over my life, I believe no organization should have been allowed to ship out children under 18 years of age. After that they have some chance to defend themselves against labour-hungry and dollar-hungry farmers.

Jack W. (Full surname withheld by request)
Lakefield, Ontario

I was one of the lucky ones.

I was only in Peterborough a few days when I went to live with people 10 miles from there. I was well treated and stayed with them for nine years—until I got married. I had come out to Canada from England in 1912 when I was 13 years old.

The people I worked for came from Toronto and were called gentlemen farmers. In the summer they ran a resort and we were very busy—up at 4.00 a.m. and working until 9.00 p.m. They had a small store and also ran the small post office. I learned how to harness a horse and drive it for the mail in the winter. I also learned how to milk cows, and feed them and the horses. I never did any farm work—only in the fall when I helped pick the potatoes. During the war years of 1914–1918 lots of girls helped out in the fields but I never did.

I think I was one of the lucky ones as I was never hurt in any way. I can say no one ever offered to hit me, for if they had I'm afraid I would have hit back. I had a very quick temper but I learned to hold back. I will say I was called quite a lot of names when the farmers got mad at me, but that didn't bother me too much. The only thing I learned to do around the house was how to cook and bake. I knew how to sew, knit, clean floors, wash dishes and clothes before I came here.

Mrs J. E. Stewart
Née Lily E. Clapham
Peterborough, Ontario

I have had my ups and downs.

We were two days ahead of the Titanic when she was struck by an iceberg with so many lives lost. The Quarrier Homes had sent out 100 boys and 100 girls on that 1912 trip. We sailed from Greenock on the Scotian. From the Brockville Distributing Home I was forwarded to a couple who were farming in Renfrew County. Later they bought a farm near Sault Ste Marie and I moved with them.

I have never regretted being in the Quarrier Homes and being brought up by their discipline to know right from wrong. I give them credit for my being where I am today. I have had my ups and downs in life but God has been good to us in giving us our health and strength.

I married in England when I was serving in World War II. She is a lovely girl and we have two of a family. The couple that adopted me are still living just a few miles from where I live and I go to see them regularly. Both are in their late 80s.

William Moir
Sault Ste Marie, Ontario

When she found me washing my clothes she would say: 'I don't pay you to fool away your time.'

I well remember getting ready to come over here. I had a metal trunk filled with new clothing—a perfect fit too, as we were measured for our clothing which was made in the large work-room in Barkingside. I had a Bible, a New Testament, a book of Bible stories and a brush and comb. I still have the three books and my brush but the comb got broken.

My father left the family when I was a small child, and I was taken to the Ever Open Door in Liverpool, England. There, in 1904, I was adopted by an aged couple named Mr and Mrs John Jenkinson. Mother, as I called her, was very kind to me. I took the place in her heart of the little four-year-old girl they lost by death. Then Mom took very ill and Mr Jenkinson had to go into the hospital so I was placed in the Girls' Village Home in Ilford, Essex. Mr Jenkinson signed a paper giving permission to send me to Canada and I arrived here in September 1911.

At Peterborough I was put on the train. My ticket was furnished by the family I was to go to help. I was 13 years old. When I reached Fenelon Falls the man met me at the station with a horse and buggy. They were so kind and I fell in love with the baby boy who was just beginning to walk. I had never seen a child try to walk before. I had a nice bedroom of my own, a good warm bed, and good food. I also went to the Anglican Sunday School. In the evening I would sometimes go to church with Mother Auldous. Father Auldous kept the baby whom they called Max.

I went to public school and had good marks in everything for a fourth grade scholar, but I knew no history or geography of Canada, so I was put in grade two. Many of the children teased me about my English words which I still use and am proud of.

The Auldouses moved out West but the Barnardo Home Council would not let me go with them so I returned to Peterborough. They sent me to work for another farmer. There were two children, one in a cradle and one running about. I didn't go to school as it was winter and I never got out much. They wouldn't let me go to church or to the Christmas concert. One night I was learning to play the organ by ear and a man knocked on the door and wanted to come in. I said 'No'. Then he put the lights out. I was so afraid I ran past him and jumped over the cradle with the baby asleep in it. Everyone laughed and said I was a baby. I got away from there and went back to Peterborough.

I then went to live near Port Hope with a widow and her married son. I walked two and a half miles to school through all sorts of weather. Twice I froze my hands on the handle of my dinner pail. They didn't buy me clothes but fixed up their old ones for me; and I had to wear kid gloves with no lining in them. I worked out in the barns on Saturdays just like a man, cleaning stables and washing the windows. Before going to school I had to fill a large box with wood for the two stoves. If I didn't, I got a good beating with a switch. I was also beaten for stealing cakes and things from the cellar. I told them I never touched them—I had only put clean paper on the shelves. One day the hired man was sorting apples in the cellar with the door open a bit, and I saw the old barn cat come out with a tart and take it to her baby kittens. I got blamed for so much and no one ever believed me.

Another day I was sent to gather eggs and heard a baby chicken peep in the shell. I never knew about them being hatched and proceeded to break the eggs so that they could all be together. They should have told me not to touch them when the eggs were breaking. Anyway, the man broke a switch off a tree and hit me all the way to the house. I was sore for a week.

Next I went to a family with four children who lived near Stirling, Ontario. The woman had been a lady's maid in England and the man was a house painter and paper hanger. They had a house, two acres of land, horse and wagon, nine cows, two pigs, and chickens. I helped to put in a large garden, got wood wherever I could find it, carried water half a mile for cooking and washing. I would clean the house from top to bottom and then sit down to eat. I often had to leave my dinner because the woman wanted something done now. She would not let me wash my clothes with the family's clothes. When she found me washing my own, she would say, 'I don't pay you to fool away your time'. I had to eat apples as she would-n't give me time to eat. One day I told the boys I was leaving and they told their dad. He slapped my face until I had a blister which formed a scab, and they wouldn't let me go to church because people would see it. I was so afraid of being beaten that I ran away. I was taken in by a kind lady who needed help but when she called the Home I was sent back to Peterborough again. The man at Stirling was fined for abusing me.

At the next place I met my husband-to-be at church. Sometimes he would drive me in the horse and buggy. He went off to war and we married when he returned. We raised four children and one we adopted.

I have always been proud of being a Dr Barnardo Home Girl. Where would I have been without their kindness?

Florence Horne
Ingersoll, Ontario

All the places I lived at were farms and I felt I was lucky that way.

The only corporal punishment I received at Stepney Causeway was that first day. I was bathed, my head gone through, my clothes taken away and others put on me. The woman dressing me put odd shoes on my feet. I remarked on it and she belted me across the face. I don't think she would have kept her job long because it was a strict rule of the Home—no physical abuse. Then we were examined naked by a doctor. I've heard people say a child never feels shame where the body is concerned. Don't you believe it.

That first night I slept in a small single bed. Right next to me a tiny mite, only three years old, was sobbing. I got out of bed and took her in with me. I was sobbing too and outside some woman in the neighbourhood was yelling 'Lily'. That was my name so you know what it would do to me. I've thought of it hundreds of times, and to go back a little farther in time, one would wonder why a mother would part with a nine-year-old. Well, it isn't for me to judge. I think many, many times my mother regretted it and paid for it in heartache. I loved my mother deeply and I can only believe what she so often told me—that she did it for the best.

Well, I was a problem to her. I played truant from school frequently. My mother worked out and I had a sister ten years older who worked out also. So I ran wild on the street. From this state of freedom to discipline you will have an idea what I went through. I'd had a glorious childhood, a few hidings which I richly deserved, but an awful lot of love and care.

At the Village Home at Ilford there were cottages with 24 girls in each one and a type of foster mother. One night a week, we were gathered together in the dining room and each child was given and shown how to mend a piece of clothing or darn a stocking. On Saturday mornings the cleaning of floors and the bigger jobs were done. We would have to wash our combs and brushes and clean out drawers. It was marvellous training really. For food, we had treacle and porridge for breakfast, some thin soup at noon with dry bread, and bread and treacle for supper. It sounds like a slim diet but the Home probably did not have the funds then, that they would have in later years. Before school every day I and another girl scrubbed a table each in the dining room. Each table seated 12, so you can guess the size. Then the floor was scrubbed on our hands and knees. And then—this I really hated—24 pairs of shoes had to be cleaned and shined five nights of the week. It was getting the mud off first that really bothered me.

We went to one big school of course and to one big church, the Church of England. Once we were sent out of England we had to go to whatever church was near to where we lived. It was required by my faith that I attend the Roman Catholic Church, but in all the five different foster homes I was in in Canada, I was never near a Roman Catholic Church.

I was 11 years old when I left England on the Corinthian in March 1912. After a week or so at the Girls' Home in Peterborough, I was sent out to a farm at Ingoldsby, Ontario, near Hamilton. I walked three miles to school—one mile of it along the lake shore. The country was beautiful and I loved it. I was fed well and never slapped or hurt. I loved the farm animals too, and had no fear of them, not even of the big ugly bull that the men led around by a chain. I worked hard there for a year and when my term was up I went to a place near Orillia. The atmosphere was not the healthiest. The older son, age 30, was something special. He went around with his eyes wide open, fortunately for me. I was just 13, but I knew something was wrong. The younger son, at 24, was a psychopath and an agnostic. He had a number of arguments with his mother and ended up slapping her. I didn't ask the Home to move me away. I suppose I felt I might get into a worse place. After all I was well fed and not abused and my contract was only for a year—not so very long.

All the places I lived on were farms and I felt I was lucky that way. The third one was at Uxbridge where I stayed for three and a half turbulent years. There were three boys in the family, all red-haired and the lady of the house was red-haired. My own hair was copper-coloured, so you can imagine the heat. I took a lot of abuse here, but as the old saying goes: 'Into each life a little rain must fall.' I didn't go back to Peterborough to be placed on the next farm. Relatives of the Uxbridge family drove 10 miles and picked me up with a horse and buggy. They had a 12-year-old daughter and a 17-year-old moronic son, and there I had to battle for a different reason. Maybe I make too much of the sex business, but I'm a good fighter that way.

There was no sex problem at the last place, thank goodness. The farm was near Lindsay, Ontario, and I worked hard in the fields and milked five or six cows morning and evening. I was paid $7.00 a month until some neighbour—I never found out who—wrote to the Home saying I should be receiving $10. Well, bad as they used me—which was getting slapped around nearly every weekend—I stayed on and helped them until November 1918. I could have left them on 2 August, when I was 18 and out of the care of the Barnardo Home.

My separation from my mother left its mark in some respects. I wouldn't go in a crowd of three until I was twenty or more, and I was sensitive to an awful degree. I married at the age of 20 and separated from my husband two years later. That was the only sad part of my life.

I'd get up on a soap box to laud Dr Barnardo any time. He was a very special person.

Lillian McFadden
London, Ontario

Why did they want me?

My father was hurt in the steel works in Sheffield, England, and later died leaving mother with seven children. My two brothers and I were put in Dr Barnardo's Home. Because I was sick my two brothers were sent out to Canada ahead of me. I followed, arriving in Quebec City in the spring of 1912. From there I went to Toronto.

After about two weeks I was put on a train for a place called Manchester, near Port Perry, Ontario. I had to change trains at Whitby Junction for the milk train to Manchester. At the station a lad of about 16 years came up, looked at my label, and said 'You come with me'. He had a horse and rig so I climbed in. I had a Barnardo trunk which he picked up. (I use it today as a tool chest, but am sorry that along the way of life I lost the Bible, the New Testament with the date I came out, and Dr Barnardo's photo.) I was taken to a farm near the village of Utica. There I met a lady, two other children, and the farmer. I thought the lady, who was very kind, was the one who was running the house, but the next day the farmer's wife arrived in a horse and buggy. I went out to meet her with the boy who had brought me from the station.

'This is the new boy' he said to his mom.

She said to me 'Take the horse and buggy and put them in the stable.'

When I told her I didn't know how, she said that I would soon learn if I stayed around.

I was used like a slave and after three years ran away. The Home man came down to look into it and I was sent to another farm. It was like being out of jail.

I was 12 when I came out and always wanted to see mother, so I joined the army at 16 and that was my first break in life. I got to England and went to see her. It was a heart-breaking experience. I brought her and my youngest sister and brother back to this country with me after the war.

One thing sticks in my mind to this day. That first farmer and his wife had two boys and a girl of their own. Why did they want me? Why? I stayed on the farm, did the work; they went to school and the oldest boy went to university. The only time I got to school was when the weather was too cold to work outside.

I am still rolling along at 70 years with my wife and 18 grandchildren.

James Wilde
Whitby, Ontario

My mother was always treated like their very own.

In 1912 when my mom, Ethel May Smith, was seven, she and her sister Dorothy, aged 11 or 12, were sent by ship to Canada. They arrived in Halifax, and there they were separated. My mother was taken by a family in Kent County, New Brunswick, who were very good to her. Later she came to Saint John to work.

After many years of separation her sister Dorothy finally reached us. I was so pleased but Mom was not as excited as I was. She was very nervous about it. My aunt Dolly came to Saint John and I arranged for them to meet for the first time in nearly 55 years. My mom finds it hard to accept her sister after so many years of absence. I am trying to understand why.

My mother remembers nothing about England—the voyage, the arrival in Halifax. Her memory seems to start when she arrived in Buctouche, New Brunswick, and the neighbours and friends all came to see the new little girl whom the Coates family were taking into their home and their hearts. My mother was always treated like their very own.

My mom has finally started to talk a bit about it all which is good, after keeping it bottled up inside over the years.

Ethel May Smith
as told by her daughter, Mrs Roberta King
Saint John, New Brunswick

EIGHT

THE YEARS
1913–1915

Few women have ever been loved as was she. I am of the opinion that
God sent her to me for a while to make me happy.

I was one of many children sent to Canada in the year 1913 by
Dr Barnardo's Home. I was 10 years of age and as one might expect I felt
carefree, without a full realization of what the future held for me. After
leaving Liverpool, we crossed the mighty Atlantic in two weeks and three
days, arriving at Saint John. From thence I was sent to 50-52 Peter Street,
Toronto. Later the Home officials placed me aboard the train that took me
to Orangeville, 49 miles away, where my future foster parents awaited me
with a horse and buggy. I met his wife and elderly sister who scanned me
as though I were some kind of freak. They passed no remarks.

I learned that the farm was spoken of as the 'Old Homestead'. It was in a
secluded area bounded by bush. Blowing sand was the order of the day, and
grasshoppers were a plague in the hot summer months. I attended public
school and that was the only joy I knew during the six years I remained with
these people—apart from the fact that I enjoyed a close association and com-
munion with my Creator. I prayed for guidance and wisdom which I received.
That has been the one factor that has helped me through the years.

My foster parents had no children of their own. I grew up without
companionship and, worse still, without parental love. They were domi-
neering and bad tempered. Their pretence to Christianity amounted to
Bible readings and family prayer which in itself was good. But it irked me
a great deal when I discovered they did not practise what they preached.

I learned more from life than I ever learned at school, though I was an
apt pupil and was considered above average for my age. However unhap-

py I was with my lot, there were compensations. Definitely the farm was a healthy place and the work extremely hard, as I was expected to accomplish the same amount of work as the adults. Hard work never harmed anyone. It is one's attitude that counts. I believe the hard training fitted me for my future and I am happy to say, has stood me in good stead.

In 1919, at the age of 16, I started out to earn my own living. I was shy and retiring at first, but adapted easily to the new life. I married at 25 the woman who made up to me for the love I did not receive as a child. She was the mother of our three children who are successfully married with children of their own. Few women have ever been loved as was she. I am of the opinion that God sent her to me for a time to make me happy. She has gone back to God, but I shall have beautiful memories for the remainder of my days and be thankful for her while she was here.

I remembered my Creator in the days of my youth, and I have never ceased to remember. Though my health is fast failing, and again I am alone and sad, I know I do not walk alone.

Name withheld by request
Toronto, Ontario

It must be awful not to have someone to call your own.

All his life my father-in-law, Frederick John Bubb, has been searching for some member of his family, but all efforts to locate them have been useless. He has a sister Ethel and a half-sister and possibly half-brothers, but he does not know where they are. The family's address when he was placed in the Middlemore Home was 96 Speedwell Road, Hay Mills, Birmingham.

Frederick Bubb was born in South Yardley, Birmingham, on July 6, 1905. His mother died in 1913 and the father remarried. There was friction between the boy and his stepmother, and he ran away from home. Apparently the father could not solve the problem between his son and his wife, and placed the boy in the Home. He sailed for Canada on the Carthaginian, arriving in Halifax May 30, 1914. He was taken by a family who had no children and who raised him and gave him a good education.

His search for his family seems so hopeless and so pitiful. It must be awful not to have someone to call your own.

Frederick John Bubb
as told by *Sylvia Bubb*
Saint John, New Brunswick

This was a lovely home where we lived a normal life.

Fifteen days after I arrived in Canada on April 15, 1913, I was five years old.

My sister and I stayed at Knowlton, Quebec for a month. Then we were both adopted into the home of Mr and Mrs George Derrick of Merrickville. This was a lovely home where we lived a normal life. I went to public school and for one year to high school. I was needed on the farm so I left school, but I loved farm life and its activities.

When I was 20 my foster father died and my mother and I came to the village to live. For two and a half years I worked as a saleslady in a general store, and then on April 2, 1932, I was married to a young farmer. Five years later we moved back to the village where we owned a successful garage business.

We had five children, three sons and two daughters. When the eldest was 20 years old my husband passed away. I have been a widow for 15 years. My family are now all married in homes of their own and I have eight lovely grandchildren.

I have lived in the same community for 57 years. When we came here we were accepted by all the relatives of our adopted parents and have always had a part in any activities.

My experiences are average. We all have our memories, both happy and sad. I know of no relatives in England, although there must be some of my generation—and younger—still there.

My sister, who was seven years older than I, passed away in 1956. I have always longed to go back to see England. I don't really know why. I guess it's just the feeling, as the poet said 'This is my own, my native Land.'

Anna Mae Telford, née Evans
Merrickville, Ontario

I was so wanting to give some poor children the love and care that they needed

Life has been good to me and my sister. We both married young. I was only 18 when I was married and my husband was 21. We had three children—boys—and we adopted a little girl. Dad and I are retired now—have been for 13 years. We sold our farms, three in all, and we still keep well.

My sister and I came to Canada in June 1914 from the Girls' Village Home—Dr Barnardo's Home in Essex. We travelled by train to

Peterborough and there my sister was placed with my younger brother in a boarding home. He had already been there for two years.

I was 14 years old and I was put out on a farm near Cookstown as a mother's help. I worked very hard in the house and barn and in the fields at harvest time. I milked cows and fed calves and hens. Then I came into the house to help get supper, wash the dishes and get three children ready for bed.

I never got any more schooling and I was paid $4.00 a month for my work. I had to buy all my clothes and the other things I needed out of that. Lots of times I worked 12 to 14 hours a day. But I wasn't the only child in this position. There were some worse off than I was.

While Dad and I were on the farm I boarded children from the Children's Aid—as many as 17 and 18 children. I was so wanting to give some poor children the love and care they needed. It is different now. The kiddies from the Children's Aid get schooling, thank God, and they are made to feel that they are as good as children with parents. Some of the children I raised from the time they were little. They got a high school education and good jobs and they think of us as Mom and Dad and come to see us just the same as our own children and grandchildren.

Mrs Mary Feldey
Cookstown, Ontario

We have been taught that God made man but I don't think He made this one.

One of the nuns came to me one day at St Charles School, Brentwood, Essex, and said 'Your mother and three of your sisters are here to see you. Come with me and I will take you to them.'

That was the first and last time I saw them. Shortly after that the nun came to me again and asked if I would like to go to Canada. She said that there were farmers who would like to have a boy like me. I was only eight at the time, and not very bright, I guess. I said 'Yes'. Not long after I was on a train. Then I was put on a ship and there the nun left me.

Then I knew that this was not just a little trip into the country. I began to cry but the ship left anyway. I landed at Quebec on the 28th of August, 1913—my birthday. There I was put on a train for Ottawa where I was taken to St George's Home, to be sent out to some farmer.

Then the day came. I was sent to a farmer in Ontario. A new life started for me in Canada and I was to be sent to school. But this should have been done in England because farmers don't have time for that. I went to school twice that I remember. Once was on a cold winter morning. The school was some distance away and by the time I got there my boots were frozen so hard and my feet were so cold that the teacher made me sit by the stove and take off my boots. There were holes in my socks and it took some time before my feet got warm. I spent most of the winter helping the farmer cut pulpwood.

We have been taught that God made man but I don't think he made this one. I spent nights rocking the cradle when other kids were sleeping. And many nights putting cattle out of the grain fields. I remember one dark night I was out there with the lantern and the stupid cows were running all over the place. One of the neighbours was up and on his way to market. In those days one had to leave early. He saw this strange light going all over the field. Thought it was some sort of ghost. They were great believers in ghosts in those days. Today people would think it was something the Russians were testing.

In those four years my outstanding friend was a dog. One day the farmer went to market about 18 or 20 miles away. On his way home he picked up a little black and white collie pup beside the road. I think it was dropped from Heaven. It turned out to be the greatest little thing God ever gave four legs to. It saved me a lot of endless running after cattle. All I had to do was call his name—'Sport'—and in no time he'd have them out of the woods. Without him I would have walked all day and got a licking to boot for taking so long.

I remember that foxes were as common as the hens in the barnyard. One day someone put out poison for the foxes and poor Sport got some of it and he died. He left some good memories behind.

At this farm I was given to understand that an orphan was the lowest type of person on earth just about and the insults I had to take even at the age of 10 or 11, have always stayed with me. It's only the bruises on the outside that I don't feel any more. I was horse-whipped, kicked, and belted around until I got so hard I could no longer feel it. I was to blame for most anything and everything. Many nights I went to bed and cried and prayed—for what I don't know. As time went on I could no longer feel the pain of abuse.

This farmer took great pride in telling me that there was no law for an Englishman in Canada. So I told him straight that one day I was going to find out. I wrote to the authorities in Ottawa. Shortly after, he was notified that I was to be returned to Ottawa at once. So that put an end to that.

After that I was sent to another farmer near Ottawa. They were a very nice family. The Missus was a school teacher. She helped me a lot in the evening with my reading and writing. I stayed with them until I was 18. Then I was free to go if I wished. I owed them more than I was ever able to pay back.

I worked from Ottawa to Halifax—back from Ontario to Calgary, Alberta. Never could stay put until I came to British Columbia. Here I have picked flowers in February. So I thought, this is the place for me.

I have always had it in my mind that if life was going to be miserable I wanted to go it alone and not share it with anyone. Every time I fell in love, my stomach would be empty. I figured if I could not keep my stomach full, how on earth could I keep anyone else's full.

Canada is a good country. It don't matter where you go. It has its ups and downs but there is no place in the world where everyone is rich like we are. So let's keep it

Michael Driscoll
Vancouver, B.C.

My Granny always regretted having done away with me so to speak...

My parents separated when I was three and I went to live with my mother's mother. Poor old Gran—she was good to me but she was in her 50s and in no condition to cope with a growing boy. I fell into ways that I shouldn't have.

Worthing-by-the-Sea was a resort town and there were all sorts of amusement machines around the pier. Farther up the beach was the band-stand and an attendant rented out deck chairs for a penny a time. Well, some bright lad found that the chairs were held together with a rod and a washer and thumb nut on each end. The washer was the size of a penny and fitted all the machines, including the chocolate dispensers. I suppose the provocation was bad enough to the man who looked after the chairs, but the people who owned the machines were losing money. The washers threw them out of balance and they were coughing up pennies along with the washers. The heavy hand of the law descended and a big six-foot bobby brought me home to Gran. After several debacles of this kind, Gran decided that the end was in sight, so with considerable urging by her friends, she put me under the care of the Dr Barnardo Home.

One morning a kindly gentleman came for me and away we went for a train ride. I was taken to Stepney where I met several other boys about my own age. We were fed and photographed and sent up to the top floor of the building to a room with a sloping ceiling. The ceiling was cracked and some of the plaster had fallen on my bed. There I, a frightened, sobbing, little boy, spent my first night among strangers. The Homes were good to us but the discipline was out of this bleeding world. There was a yardman who had the eyes of an eagle. He could spot the slightest movement when we were lined up on parade, or dirt behind the ears, or on the back of the neck, or other places difficult to see. Each group of boys was committed to various chores and odd jobs: washing the floors and the duck boards in the washrooms or shining shoes for the supervisors in a large shed just off the yard.

There were about 30 boys sleeping in my dormitory and it is only to be expected that there were many different temperaments among so many young lads. The matron had a room at the end of the dorm and at nine o'clock the lights were turned out. But there was enough light coming in through the windows for us to see our way around and get into hellery. One of my pals, a lad named Bill, slept on one side of a kid named Dance and I was on the other side. One night Bill and I pulled sheets over ourselves and paraded around Dance's bed a-moaning and a-groaning. Well, poor Dance, he reared up in bed and went into hysterics, screaming and screeching, and we couldn't get him quieted down. The matron came out of her room. She picked Dance up in her arms, trying to calm him, while Bill and I snuck into our beds. Then on came the matron with fire in her eyes. She walloped Bill and me on our behinds and sent us out to the bootblacking shed to spend some time in repentance.

In July, I and several other boys were picked for the Watt's Naval Training School which I believe was a subsidiary of the Home. Many of the boys who passed through there made the navy their career for life. However fate stepped in in the person of Kaiser Bill of Germany and there was a great flurry among all the organizations to get the children out to the colonies where they would be safe during the war.

I sailed for Canada in September 1914 along with about 70 other youngsters. We left Liverpool on the Corinthian and arrived in Quebec City on the 24th—a fast passage for those days. I was nine years old, and there were several lads younger than me.

My home in Canada was with a farmer, a Mr Fee, who lived at Cavan in Durham County, Ontario. The Home paid him $60 a year for my keep. I had to help with the chores—scrubbing the floors, washing the dishes, and cooking the breakfast. I also received a little bit of spending money for picking mustard stalks at one cent per hundred. The mustard crop was pretty good, and although I didn't amass a fortune, I kept the weed under control.

When I was 14, I left school and my stipend from the Home stopped. After that the farmer paid $125 over three years into a fund controlled by the Home. I received this money when I reached the age of 21, less any contributions I had donated after my 17th birthday. I still visit Mr Fee who gave me my first home here in Canada.

My Granny always regretted having done away with me so to speak, but in the circumstances it was the right and proper thing to do. We kept up a correspondence until the day she died. Then my mother carried on in her place until she too passed on. During World War II, I served with the Signal Corps and was stationed at various places in England. Most of my leaves were spent with my mother. We had happy times together. She loved the Isle of Man and nothing would do but I go traipsing around every little nook and cranny with her.

I hit farming at a period when it was all hard work. There wasn't any easy way of doing things like in the machine age of today, but I don't regret any of it. I've covered a large portion of the globe and I've come to the conclusion that the finest piece of property is one's own back yard.

Vernon Nelson
Peterborough, Ontario

She sent me the news that I had one more brother and two sisters, born after we were put in the Home.

Three of us—all brothers—were put in the Home when I was four years old. We lived there a while and then three of us—including the brother who was my twin—sailed for Canada on the Hesperian, March 20, 1913. I wasn't at Knowlton very long until a farmer came and picked me out of a bunch of boys waiting to be placed.

I landed on a farm about 21 miles from Knowlton, at East Bolton which is now Austin, Quebec. After six years on that farm I went to another one close by for a few more years. Then I got a position with a gentleman farmer whose name was Eric Fisher. He had a huge farm—400 acres— and he kept purebred Guernsey cattle. I started out as a teamster and worked up to foreman. Altogether I worked for Mr Fisher for 34 years. When he died and the farm was sold, I took another job five miles away and I stayed there for seven years until I retired at the age of 62.

My wife—an Irish girl—and I enjoy our life here at Goulais River. We live in a small cottage—a lovely spot—about 15 miles from Sault Ste Marie. I have a garden to keep me busy and my daughter and her husband and our four grandchildren are only 300 feet away.

One day I had a great surprise. A letter from my sister. She knew we were somewhere in Canada so she put an ad in the Salvation Army paper and my youngest brother who stayed in England answered it. She sent me the news that I had one more brother and two sisters, born after we were put in the Home. We never knew our parents, but I did have a chance to see my mother on a trip to England. She was in a Home at the age of 85.

My young days were kind of tough, in and out of one Home and another, but we had a good training and I think we boys made good Canadian citizens.

Harry Dowson
Goulais River, Ontario

Girls were scarce around Eldred.

It seems I was born in London, but my earliest recollections are of the Isle of Wight. When my grandmother died—it must have been late in 1905—I found myself being taken across to the mainland in January 1906 to the village of Otterbourne, Hants. There I was placed in the care of an elderly widow, Eliza Hoskins, whose address was Belmont Cottage. I lived with Mrs Hoskins for six years.

From Belmont Cottage I was taken to St Aldelm's Home for boys at Frome, Somerset. There were about 48 boys in the Home and I enjoyed being with the others but the discipline was strict and the food scanty. Two or three miles from the Home there was a country church; the Home supplied choir boys and I was chosen to be one. This was a welcome change. We had choir practice once a week and we had the walk out to the church twice on Sundays.

In the spring of 1913, someone asked 'Who would like to go to Canada?' I grasped the opportunity. Just a few of us were taken to Liverpool by the superintendent who showed us more affection then than at any other time. I was 14 years old and weighed all of 80 pounds.

On May 16 about 25 of us sailed on the Tunisian. We disembarked at Quebec City 10 days later and proceeded by train to Sherbrooke, Quebec, where a large house situated near the river was being used as a headquarters.

113

I was sent out to Brome County to a little place called Iron Hill. Mr and Mrs Darwin Sweet owned the farm. There I had food such as I had never seen before. I gained four pounds in the first month. However this did not last. Mrs Sweet didn't want me to attend the Church of England as they were of a different faith, so I was removed from this rather elderly couple to the Vernal family not far away at Brome Centre. I remember that one of my first jobs was to sit in the cellar taking the sprouts off the potatoes. I was so homesick as I sat down there that I cried myself sick. They couldn't understand why I should be like that, although the young wife had been a immigrant girl herself. I soon got over it, however, and made myself one of the family. My wages for the first year in Canada were $4.00 a month with board.

There were a few other English boys working on farms around the area, and I got to know one, Tom Cochrane. When I was 18 years old he and I joined the Canadian Forestry Corps in September 1917. We went overseas—leaving Halifax about 48 hours before the harbour explosion that did so much damage to the city. While I was in England I visited the elderly lady I had lived with as a boy. She died about a month later.

After the war I returned to the Vernal family, but in August 1919 my friend Tom and I went west on a harvest excursion to Manitoba. We worked there until freeze-up and then returned to Brome. The next summer we worked at Melfort, Saskatchewan.

In the spring of 1921 we headed for Prince Albert, and from there to Eldred, Saskatchewan, where we took up homesteads. I bought a team of oxen, built a log shack and broke my first land. Tom wintered with me there for three years. We bought violins which we learned to play, and we began playing for dances in the schools.

Girls were scarce around Eldred. Tom returned to Quebec and was married to the eldest Vernal daughter in 1924. I went back east too that year, stayed about eight months and then returned to my homestead in Saskatchewan. In 1928 I moved to the Debden district where I took up a quarter section of land and built again. The first year I cleared 17 acres by hand and hired a man and a tractor to break it. Oxen were no longer used at this time. I had three horses.

On February 8, 1932, Miss Evelyn Frappier became my wife. The Debden district was then, and still is, predominantly French and Catholic. I became a Catholic before we were married. Our son, Frank, was born in our log shack—14 feet by 18 feet—and our daughter, Lillian, was born in the same house. My wife and I both worked hard and had very little money, for we were married in the depths of the Depression. But gradually we got more land under cultivation and bought cattle. We milked cows for a long time and we used to board the school teacher for $15 a month. By this time we had a larger house for ourselves, and the teacher stayed in the little log house. Now my wife and I are retired and living in Debden.

On our last visit to England I returned to the village of Otterbourne. An old school chum still lives in the village and one day we went to the new school and there we found records of the days when we attended school together. Our names were there both as pupils and as choir boys. But the most interesting entry—the one that touched me most—was in the January 1912 report. The school master, Mr A. Rolfe, entered the following into the record and it is there for anyone to read: 'Three of the waifs have been taken away, namely Walter Miles...' There were two other names with mine, stricken from the school record.

I pretended to be amused but underneath I had much deeper feelings about that entry and the passing of 59 years.

Walter Henry Miles
Debden, Saskatchewan

They wanted to know what was the matter. I said it was like coming out of hell into heaven.

Late in the winter of 1914, a man came to cottage No. 24 of the Quarrier Home at Bridge-of-Weir, Scotland. I was 11 years old at that time, and my house chores were cleaning the upstairs floors and making the beds. On Saturday morning I had to have everything spotless. That meant no dust on the floors and no Bon Ami showing in the corners of the windows or on the glass anyplace.

When this man asked me if I wanted to go to Canada my answer was 'No' because my father was going to take me home when I got a little older. I forgot all about this man until sometime in March when word came to Mr Metcalfe that his boys were to go down to the stores to be fitted for clothes to go to Canada. I was in school and thought I would be given a pass to leave but I didn't get one. Some of the boys said that I'd better go anyway, so at recess in the afternoon we all went to the stores and while I was there the truant officer caught me. I told him that Mr Metcalfe said I was to go to the stores but that didn't matter. I had to go back to school with him and go before the principal and get a real good strapping. I got home late and told Mr Metcalfe my story and I will say he took up about my being strapped. He took me back to school and told the principal in no uncertain terms that he was in the wrong for strapping boys who were slated to go to Canada.

We sailed from Glasgow on the Hespernian on April 4, 1914, and landed in Halifax on April 18. We were all gathered in this shed affair and we had bread and tea before we boarded the train for Brockville. Of course we thought it was funny to see so much snow in April.

We spent a day or two at the Fairknowe Home and then we were shipped out to our future homes. Mine was at Charteris, Quebec, about seven miles out of Shawville. I arrived but there was no one there to meet me. Some man found out where I was to go so he took me to the hotel and there I met two men who were brothers-in-law to the farmer I was to work for. It was very dark and very late when they took me out to the farm by horse and buggy. I was tired when the wife showed me upstairs. The bed was not like the beds we sleep in today. It was made of lumber and it looked like a rough box only it had hinges and opened out. A straw tick made out of bags was inside with a sheet and blanket over it. I slept well. I guess I was tired.

The next morning after we had our breakfast the farmer told me I could harness the grey horse and hitch it to the express wagon and go in to Shawville to get my trunk. Now I had never had anything to do with a horse and I was not tall enough to stand and put the harness over the horse's back. I had to stand on a box, but nevertheless I got it hitched to the wagon and started out. I finally arrived at the station and inquired about my trunk. The station master asked me where the boss was. At that time I was talking very poor Canadian and didn't understand who he meant by 'the boss'. Then he explained himself and of course I told him the farmer was at home.

Now for the family. There were six children. The father was an old 'shantyman' and his wife—well, I liked her and her children, one especially. But I am sorry to say they lost him the following winter. He had pneumonia and died about Christmas time and I dug his grave. I could tell you what he went through but it would be better if I didn't. They lived in a square frame house and it only had board on the outside and no carpets on the floors and in the winter the children ran around in their bare feet.

In May after I helped to put in the spring crop we went into the bush and started to peel pulpwood. He felled the trees and I peeled the bark off the poplars. Now I was supposed to be going to school, but after the bush work we started into the hay. Everything was new to me. I'll never forget when he helped me hitch up the horses on a twelve-foot harrow and said I could go ahead and harrow the field. I almost turned the horses around on the harrow.

Then I got to school and found out that the education was somewhat the same as it was in Scotland so it didn't take me long to get onto it. While I was at school I got to know some of the boys of my own age and also Mr and Mrs Kelly who ran the store at Charteris. They were very kind to me. Many times I needed a scribbler and she would give me one. And of course I had to go to church and when they found out I could sing a little I was put in the choir.

Well, the haying was done and harvest started and he only had one very large field with a few stumps in it. I used the cradle and mowed around the field and racked up the grain in sheaves and tied them. Then when he started to use the binder he showed me how to stook and I kept up with him. The threshing started and I had to exchange work with the neighbours and sometimes the grain was terrible with smut. I would come home black with it. Later I went into the bush and skidded out poplar and after that I took one end of the cross-cut saw and he the other and we sawed up 100 cords of pulpwood and that winter we drew it into Shawville.

Now I never told you about our eating. The meals were not the best but I guess they were what they had to have. There was a half barrel of salt herring in the corner of the kitchen and a beef hanging up out in the barn. If they wanted meat I had to take the axe and bring some in. Dessert was black molasses—but I lived on it.

As I said I slept upstairs but underneath me were two rooms that were occupied by two pigs that were going to have litters. They were under there because there was no other building that was warm enough.

All this time the farmer never had to buy me clothes. I still had the clothes I brought over from the Quarrier Home. I didn't receive pay—only board, and I figured that I had about six months off to go to school in the two years I spent at Charteris.

One Sunday afternoon I went to church with another boy and the minister of the Anglican church saw me. So on Monday afternoon when I went into school he was waiting for me. He informed me that it wasn't right to go to another church but I could bring anyone to our own church. Well, I am Scotch and I told him that if there was a Presbyterian church that was the church I would be going to. I think that started my move out of Charteris.

That summer, 1916, I went back to the Quarrier Home in Brockville and around the end of July, I was sent out to Cardinal, Ontario, arriving about four o'clock in the afternoon. There I was met at the station by a beautiful school teacher, Miss Ina Mercellus, who taught school at Prescott. She was home for the summer holidays with her mother and stepfather. Those two were the best people I have ever known.

When we were about half-way home, Ina asked me if I could drive and I said 'Yes'. So she gave me the reins and stopped the horse and got out of the buggy and went into a field and picked a bouquet of Brown-eyed Susans. It was right there that I thought 'What am I getting into?'

When I arrived home, Mr Wilson, whom I later called Uncle Jack, unhitched the horse and we went into the house. I was shown my room and got ready for supper. When I sat down to the table and saw everything on it and after Uncle Jack said Grace, I started to cry. Of course they wanted to know what was the matter. I said it was like coming out of hell into heaven.

That table had everything on it that one could think of—meat, potatoes, gravy, cakes (not just one but more), about three kinds of syrup, fruit and pie. During the summer before school started all I did was get the cows at milking time, get the wood and water in, wash the dishes and do part of the housework. When that was done I would get dressed up and go with Ina to one of the neighbour's farms and play tennis. During the summer I also met my school teacher, Miss Cora Smith, who was a great help to me during my four years in public school.

Now when I came from Quebec to Ontario the standard of education was much higher. I started back at junior third, then went to senior fourth and was ready to try my entrance exams. There were four of us trying them—two girls and two boys. Miss Smith was sure one of the boys would pass and I might be a close second. One day while I was helping in the hayfield I saw her running back to where we were. She told me she had just come from Prescott where she heard I had passed and I was really overjoyed.

Then Mr and Mrs Wilson sent me on to Iroquois High School. They paid my room rent and I boarded myself, cooking my own meals. I went for two years and then I thought I would be more use at home, as Mr Wilson was getting older.

I joined the army after hearing that the Germans were trying to blow up the Firth of Forth bridge. I think I have done well to become a Canadian and I detest what our government is trying to do—in breaking away from the United Kingdom.

W. B. Cartledge
Perth, Ontario

The rest of the ship was filled with field guns and shells.

Well, my family emigrated to northern Ontario in 1905 and went back to England two years later. I think it was the cold that made my mother return.

Then in 1915 I joined the Sicilian as 1st class pantryman. We sailed on September 8, 1915, with several hundred children from the Barnardo Homes. While coming through the English Channel we were ordered to put in to Davenport. Owing to the ship only being half loaded, the rest of it was filled up with field guns and shells. Then we went over to Le Havre and unloaded the war material with the children aboard.

There were some English soldiers on the quayside. The children were looking down and talking to the soldiers and they told the children that at nine o'clock a lot of German prisoners of war would come marching past the ship. As the Germans came by the children started to sing 'God Save the King'. Then we put out to sea again.

The carpenter made an imitation wooden gun to mount on the stern of the ship to frighten away the German submarines.

Well, we buried two children on the way over. They died of pneumonia. Once we were in the St Lawrence River, Captain Peters gave a party. The children sang, a lady passenger played the piano, and we served ice cream and cookies. They went ashore at Quebec City and we went on to Montreal to pick up a large number of boys from Newfoundland. They were fishermen's sons, and were to be distributed around the British Navy as lookouts on account of their good eyesight.

G. Lebrun
Los Angeles, California

The thing that hurt me most was the fact that people would not believe me or trust me.

I was the youngest of a family of seven. When I was 10 months old my mother and father separated. My father kept the children and hired a housekeeper. She didn't stay long—so it was a succession of housekeepers and we were being neglected. Finally my mother arranged for my brother and me to be taken to the Babies' Castle of the Barnardo Homes.

I don't remember much of the next three years, except that in the afternoons after our nap we had clean bonnets to put on and were taken out to the swings to play until tea time. When I was five and my brother six, a lady took us on a train to Five Oak Green in Kent. There we were met by a middle-aged, motherly woman who took us to her home. We started to school and life was pleasant.

For three years we lived a happy, carefree life. Then in 1915 our foster mother told us she could no longer keep us. There was a war on and food was scarce so we were being sent back to London. She showed us the German zeppelins but they meant nothing to us.

We were taken to Stepney Causeway—a double house with the boys going in one door and the girls in the other. I fought and cried to go with my brother but was told I would see him in the morning. The next day he was brought into the room where I was and they went through our clothes which were all in one trunk. When this was finished they separated us and I never saw my brother again.

From Stepney I was sent to the Ilford Cottage Homes—a village made up of cottages with a house mother for each one. Because of the war it was the rule that no lights were to be seen at night. The blinds were pulled down and blankets were put over the windows. I was at the cottage about three weeks when I was told I would be going to Canada. They said that my brother would be on the next boat. Then I was taken to another building and into a room that had shelves and shelves of clothes. Here I was fitted out for Canada. My clothes were put into a small tin trunk, along with a New Testament and a book called Travellers' Guide from Life to Death.

In the meantime my father had been notified that I was sailing for Canada and could see me before I got on the boat. He didn't come, but I saw a lot of people there, hugging and kissing their children. We all got on the boat, and how many there were to a cabin I don't remember. We were told when we got out on the English Channel and out onto the ocean. I remember that one day when another ship seemed to be stopped and was sending a message to our captain. I heard some of the girls talking about it and they said our ship was to go to France as there was a German submarine in the water. So to France we went until given the 'All Clear' signal. Before we sailed again we saw some German prisoners and we all yelled 'Three cheers for the French and none for the Germans.'

Out on the ocean some of the girls got seasick and one girl threw her shoes overboard. Then one morning we were told to keep quiet. A young boy was very ill and the next day he died. He was buried at sea. I shall never forget that box, weighted with chains, being lowered into the water.

We landed at Quebec, then boarded a train for Peterborough. When I went in the door of the Home in Peterborough, a girl reached for me.

'Don't you know me?' she asked. It was one of the sisters who had lived beside us at Five Oak Green. She gave me a bath and a change of clothes and told me I would be going out to a home the next day.

The next afternoon a placard was hung around my neck and I was taken to the station. No one on the train talked to me, and I sat there like a statue. When I arrived at Coboconk it was dark. The conductor put me off and two young men picked me up, wrapped me in a blanket, and away I went for my first buggy ride. My new home was on a farm the other side of Norland. My foster mother gave me something to eat and then took me upstairs to a little room just off hers.

The next morning after breakfast she gave me a doll. I played with it and looked out the window at the lake just a few feet away from the door. When she took me out to the barnyard I was terrified of the calves and the geese hissed at me. In about a week mother took me to school—two miles along a road that had bush on each side. When winter set in, the lake froze over and my mother took me to school over the ice. It made loud noises and I thought it was cracking. After a couple of days I got brave and went to school alone. One day after Christmas a bad snowstorm came up. The teacher told me I had better leave school and start for home. I went out on the ice, but soon the storm got worse and the snow thicker and I could hardly see the shore. The snow was deep and there was no path but I made it.

Towards spring I had a letter from the Home telling me that my brother had died. I just could not believe it. When I calmed down my mother read another letter to me. It was from an older brother who had come out to Canada with a different organization. He told me that another brother, now in the army, had come with him, and he gave me their addresses. I wrote back to him at Mount Forest and mother made up a parcel for my brother who was in the army.

I was nine years old that spring. I learned about tapping trees and making maple syrup and maple sugar. I saw baby lambs for the first time, and the sheep being sheared and mother spinning their wool into yarn. When it got warmer the cows were turned out to pasture. They wandered everywhere so I was taught how to find them by their bells and I often brought them home.

During the summer I had several boat trips and I enjoyed them. Then one hot day I thought I would like to paddle in the lake. The water was cold so I put on a coat and went back into the water. Somehow the coat floated me out beyond my depth and mother had to rescue me with the boat. She wrote to the Home about that and received a ticket for me to return to Peterborough. She hadn't wished to send me back but it was no use trying to explain. I had to go.

In August I was sent to a young couple in Bradford. They met me at the station and drove me out into the country to their farm. The school was across the road from the house and the church was within walking distance. Life there wasn't good. The wife often visited her mother and would be away for weeks at a time. I was put to work scrubbing floors, cleaning stables and milking cows. In September I started to school, but the farmer told me I had to work out in the fields. When a visitor from the Home came to see me she wasn't pleased to find me alone with the man of the house. So she removed me, and sent me to an elderly couple in Lefroy. It was now December, but I started school again and I also went to Sunday School. I didn't make friends very easily. I was always called a 'Home' girl.

The work was easy for me in the village of Lefroy, except that Mr L. wasn't very well. He took a dislike to me and hit me with his walking stick anytime I was near him. I was told to stay out of his sight, but his dislike got so bad I had to be sent back to Peterborough. My next place was with an Irish family on a farm at Mono Mills. They had a sweet baby boy, six months old. Grandma and Grandpa lived in the front of the house. By this time I was beginning to resent being sent from place to place. I was discouraged and homesick. After two days of tears I was told to straighten up, so I thought it over and decided I'd better behave.

That year in November when I went to the corner for the mail, I could hear bells ringing and whistles blowing and later a neighbour came and told us that the war had ended. After that I began to hear more from my family who were still in England. My eldest brother who had been in the army got in contact with my father and mother and my sisters and it wasn't long until I received letters from my family. My dad told me that I had an aunt in Canada and she would hunt me up. She did this when I was working in a huge house in Niagara Falls. I took diphtheria while I was there and then tonsilitis. The Home arranged for me to go to Toronto to have my tonsils out, and there my aunt visited me twice.

The following summer, I visited my aunt on many weekends. She told me that when I was released by the Home that I should take my full surname so that no one would know me. Then I would get away from being called a 'Home' girl.

Between my aunt and my oldest sister, who was now living near Buffalo in New York State, my life with the Home ended. My sister took me to Hamilton to apply for a visa to enter the States, and I was turned over to her care when I was 18. I was not allowed to have my money from the Home until I was 21.

The thing that hurt me most about being a Home girl was the fact that people would not believe or trust me. The name of being a Home girl was enough for anyone. They expected the worst of you. Although I had a good background I sometimes think perhaps I am a better person for having been brought up by the Home. I was taught manners and to stand when my elders entered the room, and I always got to church. The bad part was keeping brothers and sisters apart. I have met all my family again and in that way I am luckier than some.

Name withheld by request
Norwood, Ontario

NINE

THE YEAR
1920

I put up a fuss and cried at being left alone with her husband.

Although my brother George and I were placed only 30 miles apart in the same county in Nova Scotia we did not meet again until we were grown up. I was eight years old when I arrived in Canada in May 1920 with my brothers George and Charles. Charles was the oldest and he went to a family in New Brunswick.

My first place in Canada was with a middle-aged English couple who kept me for nearly three years. I was returned to the Middlemore Home in Halifax as being 'disobedient and hard to discipline'. Actually the wife had plans of returning to England for a few years—which she did. A year or so after I went there the only son was married and for a long while she would go and spend several days with the young couple to 'help out', leaving me alone with her husband. Of course I put up a fuss and cried at being left. It was all put down to being 'spoilt and showing my temper'. Why, oh why, didn't she have sense enough to realize it was something more serious?

Things have puzzled me for many years. The lady I was with had been without her husband for four years during World War I. By the time he came home she was in her mid-40s. She may not have been interested in or desiring her husband. When I think of what old-fashioned ideas she had and how she told me nothing about sex, I can see how ignorant she was in some things. Perhaps she trusted her husband, or else never gave it a thought. Anyway I am thankful I came through those years as well as I did. Some were not so fortunate.

I feel now that more care and investigation should have been taken before placing children—but then how could the authorities find out these things? Generally speaking the neighbours wouldn't know, and if they did they wouldn't be likely to tell on people who had perhaps been their friends for years. Often the children themselves would be too frightened to tell, having received dire threats as I had.

I was broken-hearted, just the same, at being sent from the only real home I'd known, back to the Middlemore Home in Halifax. But it was the best thing that could have happened.

After a few weeks at the Home I was sent to King's County, New Brunswick, to an elderly couple. They were good to me, but sad to say he passed away the following spring and she gave up housekeeping. Then I went to live with a neighbour, a couple in their late 40s. She was the only one who ever encouraged me to get as much schooling as possible. What a shock to be told in the fall that they'd only needed me to help out through the summer when farm work was heavy, and that I was being sent a few miles away to friends of theirs.

This next family had three children—two boys, and a daughter who just a few years before had had a serious operation. She used this as a means of getting her own way, and how she used it on me! Of course we couldn't get along. We were too near of an age, and I was 'too stubborn and boy crazy' to do anything with (maybe I was), so back to Halifax I went.

Finally I went to an Anglican minister and his wife in Victoria County, New Brunswick. I was then in my early teens, and she was in her early 20s and had recently had a miscarriage. She treated me like a much younger sister, gave in to my every whim, and even took me out of school to teach me herself after I complained of my teacher's indifference. Of course she soon saw her mistake, and too late tried to correct it. She ended up by telling me some very plain truths about myself, and that really hurt for I thought very highly of her. When her husband accepted a pastorate in Sackville, I was promptly shipped back to Halifax.

There I was really on the mat. I was told that I'd had enough chances and if I didn't do well this last time that I'd be sent back to England in disgrace. Needless to say that when I was sent to Mr and Mrs John Titus, an elderly couple in King's County, in April 1927, I made up my mind to do the best I could. A good thing I did, for I soon found that Mrs Titus was hard to please and very strict, but by prayer and perseverance I stayed there for over three years. As soon as I was 18 years old, I married the couple's nephew—maybe that is why I persevered—and have never regretted it. My husband knew all about the difficult times I'd been through since I was nine or ten years old and his sympathy and understanding helped through those three hard years.

Now I wonder why, oh why, didn't the authorities take a more personal interest in the children they'd placed? I remember there was always a man who came to see me in the summer, followed in a few weeks by Mr W. Ray who at that time was in charge of Middlemore Homes in Halifax. As long as we were being decently fed and clothed and sent to school for six months of the year and getting to church or Sunday school occasionally, that seemed to be all that mattered. Perhaps there were too many of us to take up much time with each. Perhaps they didn't want to get involved personally or worse still—perhaps it was only a job to them.

I remember saying to the first lady in Nova Scotia 'How I wish I had someone to love me.'

She said 'Well we love you.'

'I never get any hugs or kisses.'

'Well we feed and clothe you, What more do you want?'

I saw to it that my own children and grandchildren got and still get lots of hugs and kisses.

Winnifred Titus, née Jordan
Toronto, Ontario

'Help required. No Englishman need apply.'

In Toronto my dreams of Canada were dashed to pieces soon after my arrival. I had been excited about coming. I sailed with a party of 143 boys and 109 girls on the Scandinavian in September 1920 and thoroughly enjoyed the long train ride from Quebec City.

Then on a sight-seeing tour of Toronto we saw some lovely parks and houses, but we also saw a sight I will never forget. We were driving through the industrial part of the city and on nearly every gate we were greeted with this sign: 'Help Required. No Englishman need apply.' On account of my English accent I remember being charged 50 cents for one ice cream cone when all the money I had was 75 cents.

I went to work on a farm for $25 the first year, for $50 for my second year and $100, the third. My pay included food, lodging and clothes. The money was kept in trust for me by the Barnardo Home until I was 21.

At 18 I started out on my own. I was paid $30 a month to work on a farm near Winchester, Ontario. I was rich! I began to play the cornet in the town band and really enjoyed life. I learned my music in the Barnardo Home on the Island of Jersey—that beauty spot of the world where I had my early education. The 1930s were grim, but I played my cornet in some good dance bands and that kept me in money.

In 1932 I obtained work in Courtauld's Rayon factory in Cornwall, and with the exception of six and a half years with the Royal Canadian Air Force Band overseas, I worked for this firm for 36 years. I retired in November, 1970.

Canada on the whole has been very good to me. It is my home and my country.

Timothy Johnson
Cornwall, Ontario

A little boy, a big country, and not a soul I could call a friend.

The big news came that we were going to Canada when I had been in Dr Barnardo's Home for about three years. At that time we learned from the school books about the wolves, Indians and snow. Boy, what a thrill! The Sicilian that we travelled on was something of a wonder, and I never gave a thought to leaving England—maybe never to see it again.

The boat trip was not too exciting, except that I fell in love for the first time. I was seasick and this girl, Lily West, maybe a year older, let me lie on deck in the sun with my head in her lap. I tried many times to find out where she went but at that time the Home would not give out such information.

We landed at Saint John, New Brunswick, in March 1920 and from there travelled what seemed to me like days and nights through bush country and snow before reaching Toronto. It was then that I began to realize what I had left in England and what I was getting into here.

We were three brothers, supposed to go to the same place, but Albert, 12 years old, went to Woodville near Lindsay, Ontario; I, 11 years, went to Watson's Corners near Fingal; and Tom, age 10, went to Comber near Leamington. That was my first big disappointment, and although Tom was only 60 miles away from me it was quite some time before I found out where my brothers were.

I don't remember anything about Toronto, but I don't think we were outside the gates until I was taken to the station and sent to St Thomas. There Mr and Mrs Horton, a childless couple, picked me up, label and all, and put me into a Dodge touring car and out into the country we went. They were in the front seat and me in the back all alone. A little boy, a big country, and not a soul I could call a friend. A lonesome and afraid boy was I. I laugh about it now, but it wasn't funny then.

W. H. Bates
Bowmanville, Ontario

I cooked wild ducks with the insides still inside.

I had quite a strange life before I came to Canada. The last time I saw my mother she told me that she was dying and that was the reason I was being sent away to Dr Barnardo's Home. When I look back, the Home was a good place but I did not like it then. All I wanted was to be back with my mother. So I ran away six times. Finally my mother died and after that I was content to stay.

Then World War I ended. We heard about the wonderful land of Canada, so I asked if I could go out. They said I could and I will never forget how happy I was.

I sailed with 150 other children on the Sicilian. We arrived in Saint John on March 28, 1920. The boat trip was great and so were the meals.

From Saint John we were sent to Peterborough to the Home for girls and from there I went to a good home in a small town called Stirling in Ontario. At least the lady of the home was real nice. But he wasn't. I didn't like the way he acted but I was afraid to say anything. I used to lock myself in my room. I wanted to leave, so they sent me back to the Home at Peterborough. I was kept in the ward for five days because I had been bad, but still I couldn't tell them why.

Then I was sent to a farm in Omemee where I had to work very hard for $8.00 a month. I never saw any money, as they used to say they didn't have it. From there I went to Clarkson near Toronto, and I was there just one month. I guess they thought I should have been an expert cook. As it was I cooked wild ducks with the insides still inside. But I was only 14 and had not done any cooking on my own.

From Omemee I went to a farm near Capetown where I stayed for three years. I had to work hard and I got $10 a month. But the man of the house was a gentleman and his wife was kind to me in her way—although in the three Christmases that I spent there I never had a Christmas dinner. I met my husband while there and was married in 1924.

Today I have four boys and two girls, all married and doing well. I have truly had a wonderful marriage. It has made up for all the heartaches of being a child who was an orphan. When my children were born, I always prayed that God would spare me until they were old enough to take care of themselves. And He has. I have always been glad my mother sent me to Dr Barnardo's Home. I was well looked after and had a good Christian training.

Gladys Jessie Simm, née Hunt
No address on letter dated December 27, 1969

I would never want my son to work like I had to, for $5.00 per month and board.

During most of World War I, I lived in a private home at Bishop Stortford. I can remember the soldiers leaving for the front lines and the wounded soldiers returning by the train load. It was also quite an experience to see the German zeppelins come over and drop their bombs. The people I stayed with, Mr and Mrs Pomminter, treated me like one of their own. I sold papers on the street and helped a florist on Saturday.

I was broken-hearted when I had to leave this home and go into Dr Stephenson's Home at Harpenden, Hertfordshire. This was a compound made up of large houses, each having about 40 to 50 boys. The discipline was strict. I will never forget our drill master, Mr Euston. If we did not do the drill right he gave us what we called 'whistle pie' on the head.

After being there for some time, I was sent to South Wales to an old hotel that had been converted into the J.A. Gibbs Home for Boys by a lady who had lost her husband in the war. Here we had the opportunity of going to Canada, Australia, or New Zealand. They showed us tempting pictures of people picking fruit, so in 1920 I chose Canada. I went under the Premier Howard Ferguson colonization scheme, sailed in August, and landed in Quebec City. From there I went on to Hamilton.

My first encounter with Mr Hills, the superintendent there, was when a few of us boys went into the peach orchard and helped ourselves. We did not know that he was sitting on the veranda looking at us through binoculars. Naturally we got a tongue lashing but the fruit did taste good. In my opinion, as a boy of 12, I thought he was quite stern, but considerate.

After a few days of adjustment I was taken to a farm at Oakland, Ontario, where I was compelled to stay until I was 18. During that time an inspector from the Home would come around every six months to see if I was being used all right or not. I was a very homesick boy and I would never want my son to work like I had to, for $5.00 per month and board. But I guess the work and discipline did not hurt me. I am still healthy.

Francis Burchett
Kitchener, Ontario

He then said 'You are very small for 11'. My heart sank, fearing he would not accept me.

I was a piper and highland dancer with a group who presented concerts to raise funds for the Barnardo Homes throughout England, and I was quite concerned as to my chances of being picked to go to Canada. Several of us had applied when volunteers were asked for at the Boys' Garden City, Woodford Bridge, Essex. Finally I was called before Dr Jim for a medical, passed it, and anxiously awaited the news to sail. On March 10, 1920, a farewell address was given at the Home, attended by the entire group of boys who lived there—732 boys in all.

The next morning was a busy one—saying our last goodbyes and leaving for Surrey commercial docks in London. I was 11 at this time and was only hoping nothing would happen to bar me from leaving the shores of England. We boarded the Sicilian around four in the afternoon. My first sight was of the tables all laid out for supper—a welcome prospect indeed. We were joined by a group of girls from the Barkingside Branch of Barnardo's, and were introduced to Mr and Mrs John Hobday who were taking the first group out after the war. We sailed that evening and had an enjoyable trip up to the last three days when we ran into thick fog. The fog horn blew day and night. While we were crossing, the ship carrying Edward, Prince of Wales, passed us on the northern horizon. He sent a wire to us.

Finally we arrived in Saint John. It was a blessing to pass through the freight shed to the awaiting train which seemed to us like a gigantic monster after riding on the English railways. Canada was blanketed with snow and was beautiful. We finally reached Toronto and I waited there in the Home on Peter Street to be placed. After three days I was sent to a Mr and Mrs Edward Hogg at Thamesville. They met me at the station with a horse and buggy. I can remember to this day Mr Hogg looking at me and asking me if I were really 11 years of age. I replied 'Yes, sir'. He then said 'You are very small for eleven'. My heart sank, fearing he would not accept me. Mr and Mrs Hogg are still alive and they are the only parents I have ever known. Their home is my home.

When Mr Hogg took me to his farm, syrup-making was in full production in early April. They had three children of their own and an older Barnardo boy who had come to them before World War I. I was introduced to the family and it was decided that I should help Mrs Hogg in the house, as I was too small for farm work. During the next year I helped Mrs Hogg who taught me how to cook, a rule practised on her own boys also. They sent me to school the following winter, but the education that I got was not very extensive.

After serving out my time I decided to educate myself at night. Not being really enthusiastic about farming but leaning towards mechanics, I studied for an engineer's certificate while working for Silverwood's dairies. In 1929 I married a Canadian girl, served with the RCAF overseas and continued my night school studies after the war. When I retired I was Head, Physical Resources, Maintenance and Construction, at the Ontario Agricultural College.

My wife and I bought a home in Florida where we spent the winters until her death in June 1970. So after 50 years in Canada I am alone again. Being left thus, I am very thankful to Mrs Hogg who took it upon herself to teach me to cook so many years ago.

Len Weston
Rockwood, Ontario

I have everything anyone could wish for except memories of a very lonely childhood.

I was two days old when my father died and my mother decided to come to Canada to work. She left me with my father's people in England. They kept me for a while and then placed me in Dr Barnardo's Home. From there at the age of 10 I sailed to Canada in September 1920. I remember many things about the Home and the boys I lived with. I had a great feeling of fear whenever I was left alone, and I had to share presents from my mother with the other boys.

After I arrived in Canada I was sent to a farm at Milton, Ontario, where I worked and went to school for two years. These people were good to me and I kept in touch with them until their deaths a few years ago. At the next farm, near Hamilton, I was not allowed to go to school although I wanted to very much. This farmer would not keep me because of my wanting to go to school and I was sent on to another farm near Kinburn.

Eventually I found work in Ottawa where my mother lived. But she had remarried and my stepfather did not welcome me.

At 18 I joined the Canadian army and had a chance to further my education. I got married in 1938 and went overseas in 1939. I remained in the army until I was pensioned in 1952 and since then I have been working as a civil servant.

My only daughter was born a few months before I went overseas and is now happily and successfully married.

I have everything anyone could wish for except some memories of a very lonely childhood. But I thank God for the opportunity I had to come to Canada.

Arthur Drape
Kingston, Ontario

They never asked us if we were happy—just to do as we were told and to marry a nice farm boy some day.

My first years in Canada affected my whole life. I have never accepted Canada as my home, even with a loving family to help. I have inwardly longed for England and the little town I lived in with 'Auntie'. Even the flowers are not the same here. When I see the lovely trilliums in the spring, I compare them with the bluebells and primroses we used to pick in the woods in England.

I was born in Liverpool. I dimly remember my father's funeral. I never found out anything about his family, and my mother's family were not interested. The only person I visit in England is my sister. She has a comfortable life, lives like most of the working class over there, and does not bother with relatives.

After my father's death my mother took me to the Sheltering Home in Liverpool. I had one sister already in the Home. My two other sisters were sent somewhere else. Apparently the older one was sent to Canada. Many years later she traced me. She was a graduate nurse in Edmonton, Alberta. She eventually moved to the United States and married a commander in the navy.

From the Liverpool Home we were taken to Stepney in London, and from there to the Girls' Village Home in Ilford, Essex. We were treated kindly there. An attractive lady whom we called 'Mother' looked after us. I remember she used to sing to us in a very sweet voice. One song she sang was about an orphan girl who died, and the words Oro Pro Nobis ran through it. We used to like her to sing that song.

My sister and I were only at the Village Home for a short time. We were sent to Halstead, also in Essex, where we were met at the station by a little, plump, rosy-cheeked woman who asked us to call her 'Auntie'. She walked us to her home which was an ivy-covered causeway house near the station. She introduced us to 'Mum', her older sister, and 'Auntie May', an invalid whom I think Auntie was paid to nurse. Auntie May was blind, and as I grew old enough, my duties were to read to her as she copied in Braille, and eventually she taught me to read Braille. I think we made them very happy. We loved all of them dearly and still cherish their memory. When we were taken from them at the end of the first World War, I never got over it. I grieved for months. My sister was able to adapt to Home life, but I never did. I wanted to die. My last memory of Auntie is seeing her dear face pressed to the train window with tears streaming down it. She wrote us lovely letters and sent us an occasional parcel, for her income was very small. In one letter she said 'I go into your room at night and kiss your pillow.' So a lovely part of our lives ended. The rest was just existing.

In March 1920 we were outfitted with clothes and a little tin trunk and put on board the Sicilian. I am not sure what port we sailed from, but I think it was Southampton. I was sick most of the voyage. We were in steerage. I still remember the rats running around, and the little bunks we slept in.

After our arrival at Saint John, we were taken to Peterborough, kept there for a week or two and then sent out to farms. My first farm home was dreadful. I was young and inexperienced, hardly knew how to wash a dish. The whole family ridiculed my accent and jeered at my clothes. The woman of the farm made no effort to help me and the old grandfather tried to make advances. I wrote to the Home, and was moved to another farm. These people were wealthy, well-educated farmers, and although they were kind, they could not be bothered with an inexperienced child. They needed someone who knew how to work, and sent me back. I moved from one farm to another and my sister was the same. Most farmers were indifferent to us and our welfare. All they wanted was cheap help and when we did not prove to be that, they sent us back to the Home. There we stayed until another place was found, meeting other young girls who were waiting like we were or who had gotten into trouble. The superintendent and his wife visited us in the sitting room briefly, but were not really interested. Actually the supervision of young and inexperienced children like us was very poor. We went from farm to farm. Occasionally some woman would call, and criticize our rooms, talk to the lady of the house and leave. They never asked us if we were happy—just to do as we were told and to marry a nice farm boy some day.

I did make a few friends, and they are still my friends. But they were mostly children of neighbouring farmers who, in some places, included me in their parties. Somehow or other we muddled through, living with different families—lonely because we were not considered one of them. If we were ill we got over it. I remember once I had a bad ear infection and with my experience now as a nurse, I still cannot understand how I avoided a mastoid infection. An operation for appendicitis finished me with one family. They couldn't be bothered if I was not able to work. I was expected to be up around six o'clock or earlier, get breakfast, and do most of the housework and cooking—after I eventually learned how. Finally, after hating every minute of living that way, I went to the city, unknown to the Home, and found a place that would give me free room and board for baby sitting in the evenings. I enrolled in business college and had enough money for a month's tuition. The Home refused to let me have what little money I had there to finish the course. I talked it over with the principal and he let me finish. When he placed me in a position with a local firm I paid him back. Actually this was the first nice thing anyone had done for me. My ambition was to train for a nurse. I had a good basic education in England, and with my business education and experience, the superintendent of the hospital accepted me. I graduated, received my degree as a registered nurse and was promoted to supervisor. Eventually I married.

Here in Canada there are still people who would look down their noses at anyone raised in a Home. That is why I concoct nice stories to inquisitive friends who wonder how I came out here. I have wept some tears writing this. Much of it I have never told my husband.

Name withheld by request

Since my guardians were older Methodist people there was neither dancing nor card games at our home.

As we boarded the ship on March 11, 1920, a telegram was read from King George V wishing us Godspeed on our journey. We were told that the King sometimes came in person to wish the children well, but at the time of our crossing he was unavailable. On board ship we sang hymns, played games, and talked about the land of ice and snow, cowboys and Indians.

After docking at Saint John we were taken by train to Peterborough where all the girls got off while the boys travelled to Toronto.

My first home was with Mr and Mrs Richard Allin of Newcastle, Ontario. My wages for the first year, at the age of 15, were $50 plus my board and clothes. A work day started at six o'clock and, generally speaking, went right through until six or six-thirty at night. In the evenings we read and chatted. Since my guardians were older Methodist people there was neither dancing nor card games at our home. However, as I matured I was allowed to attend Young People's League and community social evenings. Of course I attended church and Sunday school regularly. I spent a year and a half in public school and I completed senior fourth, as grade eight was called.

When I was in my 16th year Mr and Mrs Allin gave up farming and I went to work for her brother, Mr Albert Colwill. It was during my stay at this home that I became 18 and was on my own. However, I stayed there a total of five years and five months.

After leaving Mr Colwill I worked for another farmer who offered higher wages and easier work. However, through Mr Colwill's son (who incidentally seemed like a brother to me) I was coaxed into returning to the farm at a much higher wage. I stayed there another five years which made a total of over 10 years in the same home.

After working a year and a half for another farmer I went to manage an orchard farm and it was during that time, on November 6, 1937, that I married the granddaughter of Mr & Mrs Allin. I kept in close touch with them until their death.

Many children had unhappy times on Canadian farms, but for the most part I had pleasant experiences and a good home. I learned early in life that I must work hard and my ambition was to eventually have my own farm. This was realized in October 1938 when we purchased the farm at Newcastle where we have resided ever since.

Charles Gilkes
Newcastle, Ontario

I had a nice home with them for another three years. They took me everywhere they went.

I didn't want to come to Canada. I had a brother who came out ahead of me, but he was like a stranger. When he wrote he sent me pictures of the kind of animals he trapped for their skins.

My mother placed me in a foster home at Stansted, Essex, soon after my birth. The understanding was that I would go back to her when I was 16. I was there for 11 years and it was the only home I knew. In September 1920, I came out to Canada with a group of Barnardo children on the Scandinavian.

I was in Peterborough for a while and then I went to a farm at Carp, Ontario. They had three sons—one, a baby only nine months old. I really loved babies. I never went to school because they didn't want somebody who was going to school. I was 16 before the truant officer caught up with me. I stayed there seven years and it is still my second home.

Then I decided to go to Ottawa and maybe get into Bell Telephone. But in 1927 jobs were hard to get and I ended up as a housekeeper for a couple. He was a veterinarian and she was a music teacher. I had a nice home with them for another three years. They took me everywhere they went. One time they wanted to take me to Toronto, but I wanted to go back to Carp. They couldn't understand why anyone would give up a trip to Toronto to go to Carp.

My husband and I were married in January 1931 when times were hard. We decided to take a job working for the Hawkley Lumber Company. We went by train to Moar Lake and drove 28 miles through bush country to Rowanton above Rapides-des-Joachims. I had to make my own bread and butter and cook for four fire rangers. If anyone else decided to drive that far I would feed them too for 35 cents a meal.

From there we went to another lumber camp at Snake Creek, and then to Mattawa where my husband worked for a year or so on the Trans-Canada Highway. He joined up and went overseas when the war broke out in 1939.

I still get a little lump in my throat when I see the Royal Family. I guess it is the British in me. Canada is a good country, but you don't get something for nothing. I worked hard for everything I received, and it wasn't easy because people had the idea that Home girls couldn't be much good. Often I think of my dad. If he had lived things would have been different for me. He was a dentist and just starting up.

Mrs Norah Gray
Carleton Place, Ontario

TEN

THE YEARS
1922-1925

The farmer didn't keep me long. He hadn't reckoned on sending me to school...

Fifty years ago when I was eight years old, my mother put me in the Barnardo Home at Stepney. She was a widow and couldn't keep me properly. I was only there a few days, and was so lonely and broken-hearted at being separated from her that I ran away—but not very far. I got lost and was soon taken back. Then one day I was taken over to the Island of Jersey. When I look back I realize that it was a lovely place to live—so peaceful and quiet. The Home there was situated on a road running north from the sea-shore village of Gorey.

Well, after a while I began to settle down. I went to a school about half a mile from the Home where we were taught both English and French which was the Island's native tongue. Most of us had chores to do. I remember all our beds in the dormitories being so well made and the floors so highly polished that it looked like a show-room. Each bed spread was a light blue and inscribed in a circle was 'Dr Barnardo's Homes'. They were very strict in this Home and did not spare the rod. I got my fair share of it. I suppose we were fed enough to be healthy, but we always had big appetites so I can't say my belly was always happy. There were none of those extras we got at home when we felt hungry.

I mixed well with the other boys at Jersey and was enjoying life. Then one day on our way to school, three other boys tried to interest me in running away. They goaded me so much that for the sake of my pride I had to give in. So, one evening after tea the four of us left the playing field and crossed the fields. Soon it was dark and I guess we were lost and scared, so we went to a private home along the sea-shore and told the owners who we were and that we had run away. They were kind, retired, English people and they got in touch with the Home. While we were waiting for the headmaster, a Mr Armitage, to come and pick us up in his motorcycle and side car, they gave us hot cocoa and biscuits. I slept in my dormitory that night but the next morning I was taken to a separate building that served as a hospital, and put in a small room there. The window was whitewashed so I couldn't see out. I was given just a night shirt to wear and I spent seven days locked in this room with only a glass of water and dry bread to eat, three times a day.

The evening of the first day I was taken to the dining room where we gathered before bedtime for evening prayer. After this the black list was read and as the names were called each boy walked to the front and was given whacks on the hand or behind with a cane—and hard too. Mine was the capital crime of all. I had been singled out as the ringleader of the runaways. I was spread-eagled over the end of the table, held by four of the biggest boys, and given six strokes of the cane over the bare bottom. I was hit so hard that the first one numbed me and I never felt the other five until I was taken back to my room. I was popular and a hero in the eyes of the other boys after that.

When a few of us from Jersey were selected for Canada, I returned to England and went into the big Home at Woodford Bridge. It was like a park with a main dining hall and cottages scattered around. We were scheduled to go in late spring or early summer but measles broke out and we were quarantined for some time. I remember that while we were at Woodford Bridge we were invited to the Girls' Home. It couldn't have been far away as it did not take long to go by bus. I suppose you would call it a garden party. We lined up for nice sandwiches, cake, cookies and a drink of some sort. Then we ran back for more, fibbing that we hadn't had any yet. We had a great time chasing the girls and playing games. It was an exciting day.

Then one day in September we left on our journey to Canada. We sailed from Plymouth. My mother came down to see me off. I think that was the only time she visited me and with the sight of her came the old longing to be back with her again.

We sailed at noon. Six hours out I started to get seasick, and believe it or not, I never ate one scrap of food the whole voyage. I was so sick, but still I was made to go to the dining room and sit down with the others and look at the best food I had ever seen in my life.

I was able to walk off the ship at Quebec on wobbly legs. I believe the ship was Minnedosa and our date of landing was September 22, 1922. From Quebec we went by train to Toronto and then by bus to 531 Jarvis

Street. We were only there a few days. My first farm was at Georgetown, but the farmer didn't keep me long. He hadn't reckoned on sending me to school so sent me back. Then I was sent to a farmer down near Dunnville where I stayed for two years. I liked farm life, but couldn't take it seriously as a living. The farmer was sorry to see me go and even bought me a new suit when I left. The following Christmas he sent me ice skates which I nailed on an old pair of boots.

My next stop was a farm up near Ottawa, about 27 miles west of the city. This man was hard to work for. He had a large farm, plus another some three miles away near the Ottawa River where he kept young cattle to fatten them up for the butcher. I was still only 13 when I went there. He was supposed to send me to school but he kept me at home and made me work. His hired men would never stay long. His own children never worked, but went to school. I was treated different. I felt like a slave, as he used to threaten me with a horse whip to get me to work harder. In summer I was up at four-thirty in the morning and worked until eight or nine at night. I planned to run away. By this time he had another Home boy— a strapping, big, 16-year-old Scotch boy. He didn't like the farmer either so we ran away together. I just had old loose-fitting clothes that the farmer had worn himself and that is what I ran away in. It was a Sunday when we left. The farmer and his family had gone away for the day and left us to keep stirring the milk in the vats every 20 minutes. We walked 13 miles before sunset along the railway tracks. A train came along and stopped where we were resting beside a water tower. The engineer invited me up for a ride, but the Scotch boy said he would go back to the authorities that brought him over.

So at 14, I was on my own and got rides on trains all the way to Saskatchewan where I worked 12 hours a day for a man's pay. Then I came east and worked in the north country until war broke out. I went overseas in July 1940, and at the end of the war in 1946 I married a Canadian girl. She died in February 1959 and left me with three children. I had an awful time on my own for five years but they are grown up now.

When I ran away years ago I changed my name to hide my identity. My real name was Reginald R. Greengrass, but I am now known as Charles R. Morris, a name that was made legal long ago.

Charles R. Morris, ne Greengrass
Willowdale, Ontario

He called me a silly bastard and when I asked him what that
meant, he said I'd had no father.

My story really starts before I was born. My mother came from a well-known and haughty family, and when she became pregnant without benefit of a wedding ring, she was turned out and had to fend for herself. It made her bitter and very vindictive towards me. So as soon as I was born I was put out to board with an old great-aunt who was quite a drinker.

At the age of two my mother moved me to a convent run by the nuns of the Church of England. I was there till about age nine and I had a good school record. In the meantime mother had married a Jewish man and had another baby, my sister, a few months later. When I was nine, my stepfather took me to live with them. I loved my sister but could never understand why I got beaten so much and yelled at, and they were always praising her. But I never turned against her.

Every holiday I was sent to the Salvation Army country camp on the seaside. At times it seemed I spent half a year at each place. In the meantime my mother's youngest sister came to Canada and got married. My grandfather died and grandma went to Canada, and when my aunt wrote the Salvation Army to ask for me to come over and work on the farm, they asked my mother and she said 'Yes'. I was taken to the Army Home and there I stayed until I left for Canada in October 1922. I was 12 and had my birthday two days before we landed in Canada. I was escorted by a Salvation Army lady, a Mrs Adams. A Salvation Army man met me at Quebec, Montreal and Toronto.

My aunt was supposed to meet me in Stratford, but she was not there. I never felt so lost and lonely in my life as I did that Saturday noon, standing on the open, empty station platform all alone. The station master asked me where I was going. I didn't know, but my uncle's mother lived in Stratford and I had her address. The Travellers' Aid took me around there. My aunt and uncle came into town that afternoon. They got the letter from the Army the following Monday, saying I was coming.

Well, needless to say, life on a farm was very different. I had never been close to a cow before and was terrified of them and of the horses, pigs and goats. My two small cousins were raised on goat's milk. Within a month I was hand-milking seven cows, night and morning, feeding calves, doing separating, carrying cream cans down to the road, and getting breakfast for my aunt, uncle, cousins, a hired man who was 16, and uncle's half-witted old brother who was 72. I had to get up at six in the winter and at five in summer and have all the barn work done and breakfast ready by seven-thirty. Then I would call my aunt.

School was out of the question. I never went to school past the age of 11 years, 11 months.

It didn't take long to find that auntie was a vicious woman. She was only 22 and uncle was 45. I realize now that she must have been unhappy with him, but she didn't take it out on her children—only on me. Well, I was an innocent child and didn't know a thing about sex and I couldn't understand why my aunt would lock herself with a neighbour man in her bedroom for hours when uncle was away for a day or two with cattle. When I asked her why she locked the door, she said she would kill me if I ever told anyone. Life wasn't very good, but then it never had been. I always thought other children were better off than me. I would crawl into bed at night so tired that I fell asleep right away. But through it all I survived and grew fat and strong and tall.

Then in June 1924 my aunt went to England and took one cousin with her. I had all the housework to do as well as barn and field work. My grandmother was working in Woodstock those two years and when she phoned to see how I was getting on, she became worried. She told my uncle to get another woman to help me. He promised to, but he didn't. Then one day he caught me in the barn and held me close to him, and took me up in the hay-mow and raped me. I was terribly upset and cried a lot. He called me a silly bastard, and when I asked him what that meant, he said I had no father and that I'd grow up to be a whore like my mother. Nobody will ever know what that awful thing did to me.

My aunt came back in October and just before that grandmother found out that I had done all that summer's work without help, including feeding 14 men for four days through the threshing. She booked passage for me to go back to England with her by boat. The Salvation Army came out to see how I was about every three months, and grandma got special permission from them to take me home.

In England the Army got me a job in service to a banker and his crippled wife. I stayed there two years and saved my money and came back to Canada at the age of 16. I got a job in London, Ontario, in service and was married two months before I was 17.

Of course things were not always bad on the farm. I loved the church on Sunday, the quilting bees, the church socials and the picnics. I grew to love the change of seasons in Canada, and the countryside and all the animals and even the hard work, until that day in the barn. Then I almost hated the world and all in it. But I don't have the capacity for deep hate, thank God, or I'm sure I would have gone under. By the way, I still have high regard for the Salvation Army. Some of my happiest memories are of those kind people.

Name withheld.

There are a lot of funny little things I often recall, like plodding to school all alone, on the awful sticky clay roadside...

I will always have a good word for the care that people at Dr Barnardo's Home gave me. They brought me to Canada in April 1925 and I was placed with foster parents at Uxbridge, Ontario, where I attended a country school. After a couple of years I was sent to another home in Norwood—a change which I did not enjoy. I had to make new friends again at a different school with different teachers. I was lonely and lost.

From there I was taken to a foster home near Brantford where there were three small children. This was home to me and I was one of the family immediately. I finished my public schooling there but the break came when I was told I had to start earning my own living. I was heart-broken when I was not allowed one day in a high school and had to leave that lovely home. I was sent to Wooler where I now reside.

I came to a couple who had no family and I was accepted as their own. I had a very busy life helping on the farm for many years. I met my first husband and married him there. We moved away and had two sons.

My husband died very suddenly at an early age. My present husband whom I had known before either of us were married, came to see me after we had both lost our partners. He brought me back to Wooler and we are happy here. Once more I feel I have a good home and really belong.

There are a lot of funny little things I often recall, like plodding to school, all alone, on the awful sticky clay roads—and writing my entrance exams in a huge school, where I did not know a soul and I was so scared. The kids made fun of my English accent when I first arrived, and laughed at the different clothes I wore, which did not always fit properly. I remember too, sitting in a corner with my left hand tied behind my back, while I tried to write with my right hand. I had never done that before because of a finger amputation on my right hand caused by an accident when I was four years old.

There are many other incidents but this will give you some idea of my life in a new land which, I am happy to say, is my home now.

Mrs Lloyd Dorland, née Vera A. Coote,
Wooler, Ontario

I'm going home, back to my mother, and if you try to bring me back I will burn down your barn.

My father was an insurance agent and jeweller combined and we had a good middle-class home in England. He died when I was 12, leaving my mother with three of us children to support. This she did very well but as time went on I kept getting this urge to go to Canada. My mother said I would have to go in care of someone, and this turned out to be the Middlemore Home. So I came to Canada of my own free will and my mother paid for my care in the Home and for my passage to this country.

I entered the Home in 1923 and expected to go to Canada the next year—but the British government enacted a law whereby no children could be sent out of the country as emigrants until they were 14. This almost broke my heart for it meant that I had to wait another year. Finally in June 1925 we got word that we would be leaving England in July.

The next month was an exciting and hectic time for those of us chosen to go. All the other children in the Home were envious. We had our own bags with our names stencilled in big letters on the outside. There were 14 of us—boys and girls—boarding the train in Birmingham with the boys' matron in charge. We arrived at the docks in Southampton practically alongside the Andania, the ship we were to sail on. Such excitement. We were wild. I remember matron would shout 'Boys' and that would tone things down. My mother was on the dock to wish me 'Godspeed'. She gave me a gold signet ring with these words engraved inside: 'Love from Mother, May 1925'. I still have and treasure it. Anyway we set sail and I shouted to my mother that I'd see her in 10 years.

The first part of the voyage was lovely. We all lay out on deck and got a good suntan—but I, lucky Fred, got scorched and my face broke out in blisters. The doctor put salve on it to try to heal it and I made it worse by picking at the skin.

After about five days out to sea we hit some very rough weather. The waves came over the bow of the ship and washed the deck and crashed against the superstructure with a resounding roar. No one was allowed on deck but—well, I had to see the sight and I climbed up to the first-class deck. Looking out a window wasn't good enough for me. I had to unlock the door and go outside. I was having a grand time standing just below the bridge watching, when all of a sudden the ship gave a lunge forward and so did I. I went crashing down to the lower main deck. I faintly remember the commotion and someone saying to get me down to the hospital quick before everyone got washed overboard. I spent the rest of the trip in the ship's hospital.

So when it came time to go through immigration at Halifax I appeared blistered and scorched with a great bandage around my head. The officials simply refused to land me. I had to stay in the quarantine hospital for about a month. I had the best to eat and was allowed the freedom of the building during the day but at night they locked me in my hospital room. When Mr Ray from the Middlemore Home in Fairview came, I was released to his care. What a Godsend this man proved to be to me, and no doubt to many other boys. I stayed with him and his wife for a few days. Then he said he had a nice place for me and put me on the train for Pictou. I arrived and the farmer couldn't help but spot me right away, for I had on short pants with bare knees and a bag with my name stencilled on the side. He took me to his farm near Alma, Pictou County, where I was to work for him until I was 21 at the starting wage of $6.00 per month.

Well, it was a lovely clean home and they fed me good but that's the most I can say for them, for they had no heart whatsoever and didn't know what to expect of a young boy of 14. I was very lonesome alone out there and he didn't help matters by dogging and ridiculing me constantly. He would ask me to get a whiffletree and I wouldn't know what he meant because I was from the city and as green as a cabbage. Then he would go off his rocker and call me all sorts of names and I wasn't used to that. Once he threatened to horsewhip me for stumbling his horse, for he dearly loved his horses.

Fall came and I can remember it as though it was yesterday for it was October 7, my birthday. It had snowed about six inches in the night and the apples hadn't been picked yet so he sent me into the orchard with a ladder to pick all the apples off the trees and be quick about it. I had on short pants and no mitts and it wasn't long until I was crying with the cold but I dared not leave. I swore then and there that if I ever got the opportunity I would run away. I couldn't write to Mr Ray for I had no money for a stamp. I didn't see any of the money I earned and I earned plenty. The farmer was road supervisor of that district and I know darned well that he used to put my time in to the government as a man, at $1.00 per day. We would do a lot of work scraping the road with horse-drawn scrapers and I would follow along and throw the rocks off the road.

October rolled around and we did the fall ploughing. Then came November 1—election day in Nova Scotia and Mackenzie King was making a strong bid for office. The boss and his wife were going off to vote and he came to me and told me to take a shovel and dig a ditch to drain the water off the ploughed ground. Then he hitched the horse in the carriage and away they went to vote for Mackenzie King. Just as soon as they got out of sight around the bend of the road I beat it for the house. I stuffed my things into my bag and wrote a short note: 'I'm going home, back to my mother, and if you try to bring me back I will burn down your barn. Goodbye.'

And away I ran. I can't for the life of me remember how I got to Halifax but I got there by dark and found my way to the docks. I saw this ship all lit up and I stole up the gangplank and hid behind the smoke stack where it was warm. I stayed there about two hours but it was too hot, so I decided to look for another place to hide. Then I ran into this big coloured man. He told me this ship wasn't headed for England but for the West Indies. He pointed out another ship loading for England, and sent me off with the biggest cheese sandwich I had ever seen in my life.

It was an open wharf with oil barrels all over the deck. I settled down behind them and watched the gangway of the ship, ready to steal aboard. I didn't get a chance because there was a night watchman patrolling the dock and watching the gangway constantly. So I settled down between the barrels to wait. In the morning when I stood up to stretch a mounted policeman put his hand on my shoulder and took me off to the Middlemore Home.

Mr Ray met me with open arms. I told him how much I wanted to go home and he was kind and understanding about it. He suggested that I stay with him over the winter and then he would see. So I spent a pleasant winter with him and when spring came he told me he had another place he would like me to try out. I said I would try it and I'm glad I did.

This time I was sent to a Mr and Mrs Smith just three miles outside of Saint John. He wanted a boy to help him on his milk route and do the chores and be generally useful. My wages were $8.00 per month. I was to save $6.00 and have 25 cents a week to go to the show every Saturday night. This was a delightful home for me. The Smiths had three sons in their 20s and 30s who were really like brothers to me, and another boy from the Middlemore Home who had grown up to 18 and was considered too big for a milk-route boy. His name was Harry Fox. He married Mr Smith's granddaughter and is a mechanic by trade.

I was so happy there. Old Mrs Smith was just like a mother to me. She knit my mitts and socks and darned them and gave me heck if I didn't change into clean clothes regularly. And could she cook, especially buckwheat pancakes! The old fellow was very abrupt and sarcastic but he had a heart as big as a bucket. He kept 25 to 30 head of cattle and we all did the milking by hand. Pasteurizing was not compulsory and we used to bottle the milk ourselves and deliver it to our customers in town every day Sunday included—for 10 cents a quart.

In the evening when our work was done and we'd had supper we could do as we liked. We would all skate or ski on home-made skis and swim in the summer. Saturday nights we would hitch up the horse to the milk wagon or sleigh and go to town, put the horse in a barn there, go to the show together and then all drive home. I was always accepted by the older boys—never considered too young for them. On bad nights the old man would love to get out the cards or the crokinole board. He was a cracker-jack at that. What pleasant memories I have of those days.

Well, those years were the roaring 20s and I was growing up and getting very restless. I had the strongest urge to go west on the harvest excursions that used to go from the maritimes. I had in the back of my mind getting a quarter section of land out there and then another until I owned my own spread. Between them, Mr Smith and Mr Ray decided to let me go if I wanted to. I didn't get west but for the next two years I worked all over the maritimes. In between jobs I would always return to the Smiths and they would give me a good scrubbing, darn my socks, and mend my clothes and feed me. I would make myself useful and then go off again.

When I was working in the Atlantic Sugar Refinery in Saint John I got to know some Irish boys at the boarding house. They were going off to New York to join the police force. I decided that if they could get along in New York I could too, so I jumped the border and headed for New York. What a city! I did the whole bit—shows and everything until I had practically spent all my money and had to look for a job. I was walking the streets one day and bumped into one of the Irish boys from Saint John, now a cop out walking his beat. He sent me to an employment agency on Sixth Avenue. There I saw a job for a dairyman and poultryman combined for an estate on Long Island. The superintendent thought I was too young but finally agreed to try me for a month. This was a fabulous place—the Diebold Estate—self-sustaining, with a mansion, greenhouses and gardens, an orchard and stable, and—what interested me most—a lovely barn with just two cows and a tiled dairy, fully equipped with steam sterilizers, electric refrigerators and separator. The job was a picnic. I could do it with my eyes shut. Just two cows to milk for fresh milk and butter and 50 hens for fresh eggs.

I was there about a month when one Sunday morning this man and woman walked into the dairy. I was all decked out in my whites: overalls, wedge hat, and shoes. He complimented me on the job I had been doing and after that first morning he came to see me regularly. I told him I would like to raise some broilers and he told me to go right ahead. I got 200-odd chicks and a brooder stove and had great success. I don't suppose I lost three.

The summer went on and in the fall I heard that the boss and his wife were going to Florida for the winter. This made me feel bad, for I had poured out my heart to this man at different times and he always understood. When he told me he was going off for the winter, I said that I had a longing to travel too—back to England to see my mother. He thought that was great news and put a $100 bill into my hand when we shook hands. I promised to return there but I never did.

I went to Halifax and booked my passage home. Mr Ray made a bet of $5.00 with me that I wouldn't stay in England any longer than six months. I stayed for almost a year and had a wonderful reunion with my mother, but couldn't settle down. One day she offered to pay my way back to Canada as a present for my 21st birthday. This pleased me very much and soon I was back in Canada, the land I had learned to love. I went immediately to see Mr Ray and found to my sorrow he had died. Then I proceeded to my old home, the Smiths, near Saint John, and he gave me a job. These were the years of the Depression and jobs were hard to come by.

While I was at this job I met a girl in Saint John and I started to court her. She was an English girl who had come to Canada a couple of years before. We courted for about two years and the Smiths always asked her out to spend Sundays. Eventually we got married on nothing, and had the next 10 years of very rough going. I built a log cabin in the woods near the Smiths and they did all they could to help us. When the war started I joined the Longshoremen's Union where the government said I must stay, shipping supplies overseas. I have been there ever since. I have 28 years of service in, and still going strong. We own our own house and have raised six children—all married and doing well.

Fred Sanders
Saint John, New Brunswick

At that time the postage on a letter was three cents and that was the price of a bushel of oats.

I was born and raised a Cockney. Before my 17th birthday I was offered the chance to come to Canada under the Canadian government scheme of assisted passage for boys wishing to emigrate to Canada. This plan was rather good in my estimation. The requirements were very simple. The boy had to be sponsored by a Canadian citizen. He had to be physically fit and mentally alert. The Canadian authorities decided on the doctor to do the examination and the boy paid the fee. (In my case it cost me two shillings and six pence). The boy paid at least 25 per cent of his fare from the port of embarkation to his destination in Canada and the government paid the other 75 per cent on a loan basis. There was a period of six months before the first payment became due, and I believe full payment was to be made by the end of two years. Another requirement was to have at least $25 on landing in Canada. I changed my English money into Canadian currency the day before I left, at a money-changer's place in Charing Cross. The chap gave me $25 in silver to carry. I smile every time I think of it.

I sailed on 13 September 1923 from Southampton for Quebec City on the Minnedosa. On arrival I went by train to Medicine Hat, Alberta, and then to Manyberries, a cow town some 75 miles to the southwest. How the town got its name, I have often wondered. There were some farms in the area but mainly it was ranching country. My sponsors were an elderly couple, Mr and Mrs John Cove. They had a quarter section that they homesteaded, and they made their living by supplying the town people with milk, cream, butter, eggs and table fowl. I did the chores for them from early October until the following April. I got my board and lodging and a couple of dollars occasionally.

Then I went to work for a Swede, Axel Anderson, and helped him to build dams in some of the ravines on the ranch of a Mr Charlie Archer. When the dams were completed my employer took on a sub-contract, building the railway bed on a portion of the Canadian Pacific Railway line from Climax to Val Marie in southern Saskatchewan. That winter I loaded rails for the track-laying gang. I was the only English-speaking person on this job. The rest were newly-arrived Norwegians or Belgians—older men who had settled in St Boniface, Manitoba.

Every time I received a pay cheque I endorsed it and sent it in to the government as repayment on the loan. It was fully repaid in less than a year. I used to leave it to my employer to pay me what he considered I was worth—for I was a city boy with no experience on the farm. I must say that I was treated fairly.

When the Depression and drought years came to the prairies I had been working for Mr H. R. Woodley at Imperial, Saskatchewan, for several years. This farm was my Canadian home away from home. Mr Woodley had been paying me top wages, $50 to $60 a month depending on the crop—with room and board. The first year of depression and drought came and my wages dropped to $40 per month. The following year they were less and the third year, things were so bad I worked for almost nothing.

In March 1932 I got married. We pooled our resources and gathered together four horses, a yearling heifer, a wagon and hay rack, a set of harrows and a set of discs. Neighbours gave us a pig and four hens. One morning I loaded everything—except the heifer—onto the wagon and hay rack, and my wife and I spent our honeymoon travelling north to St Brieux, Saskatchewan, where we had arranged to take over a quarter section from my wife's brother. The dust was blowing when we left the prairies and before we reached our destination we ran into very deep snow and subzero weather. It was 30 below the day we reached our new home—a log cabin in the bush.

Well, we learned to do without and to improvise. We grew our own vegetables, butchered our own beef and pork. We learned to cure and smoke our own hams and bacon, to tan a hide for leather and to make and repair harness. From the parts of an old binder I made a rope-making machine, using binder twine for the rope. My wife made her own soap and butter and canned Saskatoon berries, chokecherries, and wild high-bush cranberries. Money was almost nonexistent. We bartered butter and eggs for groceries. Instead of paying taxes, I undertook to keep about three miles of road in repair. It was a hard, hard life, but sometimes when my wife and I reminisce we laugh about the things we did to make ends meet.

Our first crop of grain was exceptionally good. The wheat averaged over 50 bushels to the acre and the oats around 70 bushels per acre. The price—that is a different story. The average price I received for the wheat was 19 cents per bushel and the oats—well, at that time the postage on a letter was three cents and that was the price of a bushel of oats. So we fed the animals well.

This way of life came to an end in 1940. In June I joined the armed forces, and in the fall of the same year my wife sold the farm. When I was sent overseas my wife returned to Belleville, Ontario, to be with her people. We have continued to reside in Hastings County ever since.

Ernest H. Harvey
Frankford, Ontario

I was told it was a lovely farm. Boy, what a jolt I got.

This story goes back to when I was pretty young—hardly able to blow my own nose, as the saying goes. I was born in the family home at 48 Rainham Road, at Chatham, Kent, on December 2, 1910. This goes for my two sisters and my younger brother too. I remember when my brother was born. The doctor came, we were sent out of the room, and the next thing I knew there was a baby in the house. My father was away at sea. At that time he was an Engineer Lieutenant in the Royal Navy.

Our family started to break up when my mother died in February 1920. Father was at sea when she died and did not get home for the funeral or at any time after. My oldest sister—who had been disowned because she had married against father's wishes—came home and took care of the rest of us. After a while I was sent to a boarding school—Kings School, Rochester, Kent. My father must have done this by correspondence, as we never saw him. After two years things changed. My second sister, myself and my brother were sent to live with an aunt at Bush Hill Park near Enfield, Middlesex. I went to Winchmore High Collegiate School another snob school and this is where I had to get down to work to study for the Naval Academy exams. From then on it was no holidays for me, and special teachers and drill after school was out. After two years of this I was asked to appear before the Secretary to the First Lord of the Admiralty. My aunt took me to London for this ordeal. Boy, all those men in their uniforms and braids and medals. They seemed to ask me questions all at the same time.

Some time went by and then I was back in London for the final exam. I failed one paper. So that ended my father's dream that I, his eldest son, would follow in his steps and attend Dartmouth Naval College. I was taken out of school and I guess the wheels started to turn to get me out of his sight forever.

All of a sudden my bags were packed and I was sent to Hadleigh in Essex to get training in farm work at the Salvation Army's farm. This was a six-week training period and I must say that I enjoyed it. It covered everything from weeding turnips to milking cows. We were given pocket money each Saturday. I can't remember how much, but it was enough for candy and to go to the cinema.

Well, time drew close for our sailing to Canada. We were sent home for a few days to see our families. This did not mean much to me. I saw my sisters and brother but I can't remember saying goodbye to them for the last time.

Back at Hadleigh I had my father's kit bag packed with clothes and the Salvation Army gave us each a suitcase full of clothes and books—including a Bible which I still have. Then off to Canada. The voyage from Southampton to Quebec City took eight days, and the last part of the journey, up the St Lawrence River, seemed lovely to me. The first thing that impressed me—being 14 years old at the time—was the size of the ice cream cones. So much bigger than the English ones.

We stayed at the Salvation Army hostel overnight and next morning the 14 of us were all marched to the Canadian National station, bag and baggage. We had our own car on the train—one of the old type where the seats slid out to make a bed. There were no covers and I don't think I got out of my clothes until we reached Vancouver. Our meals were cooked in the coach at one end: beans morning, noon and night. Oh, well, it didn't do me any harm. In spite of it, I still like beans.

At various stops boys were put off in charge of a Salvation Army officer, I guess for work on the farms. By the time we arrived in Vancouver there were six of us. We were taken to one hostel for breakfast and then to another hostel where we were given rooms. From time to time we were assembled in an office where farmers from the Fraser Valley came to pick out a boy. I was the third one to go. I was told it was a lovely farm I'd be going to. Boy, what a jolt I got.

The next day I was put on a train for Dewdney—a whistle stop up the valley. It was pitch dark when I arrived. The train went past the stop about half a mile or so, and I was put off on the side of the track, kit bag and suitcase, 14 years old, and all by myself. I didn't know which way to go. There were no lights to guide me. I believe I cried.

In the distance I heard someone calling. I headed down the track and finally there they were, waiting. They took me with them, not to the house but out to the barn and up to the hay loft where he dug a hole in the hay for a bed. This was to be my sleeping quarters, clothes closet and all, for six months. I guess what woke me up in the morning were the cow bells. Up I got, still in the clothes I had arrived in, and down the ladder. Lo and behold there were about 20 cows in the barn and the farmer and his wife were milking. He was 60 and she was 22. She had come from a very strict family, so I guess she grabbed what she could. She did pretty well and raised three daughters for him.

From now on it was work—seven days a week—daylight to dark. I learned everything from milking to silo-filling. I was never allowed off the farm. My hair grew down to my shoulders. Finally after about a year he gave me a quarter and sent me to the local store at Dewdney where a man cut hair. Boy, did the local fellows laugh at me!

Some things stand out in my mind quite vividly. I was so hungry that often I used to go out to the field—even after a meal—and pull a turnip or a carrot, or a cabbage—whatever was handy, and eat it. I guess it didn't do me any harm because I got to be strong and healthy and I still am.

So after two years he told me he was letting me go. The day I left he told me he didn't have the money to pay me. I had not had a penny in all that time and I should have been getting $10 a month and my board. He produced three sheets of paper. On them was everything he had ever bought me. Well, out of $240 I was left $70. Three times I went back to collect my money. Each time I got a few dollars.

From this place the Salvation Army sent me over to Vancouver Island to another farm. These people were French and very good to me—but tough. She was big as a house and, man, was she the boss. He was tall and slim and quiet. They ran a retail delivery milk route, door to door in Ladysmith. I had to learn who all the customers were and what they wanted each day. It was interesting work, but about a year later they told me they were selling out and the new owners wouldn't need me, so I went to another farm, still on the Island. This time I worked for a Scot and these people treated me like a son. They took me everywhere they went and gave me time off when the work was caught up. I even had a holiday once in a while and extra money above my wages. I stayed about a year—until I had this urge to get back to the mainland, so away I went.

Now I was on my own. The Salvation Army had done their part so it was up to me to look after myself from then on. I went back to Dewdney, got a job right away and stayed for 17 years. I met lots of people this time and was right in with the bunch. We had a young people's group in the United Church and we made our own fun. Nobody had cars during those years of the Depression. Then as time passed the group seemed to break up as one and another got married and moved away.

My wife and I were married in 1937. I managed a farm for a while and then we got one of our own. Stayed with it for three years, but prices were low. We couldn't afford help and it darn near killed us both. So we gave up farming and never went back to it. I got mill work then at 40 cents an hour. This seemed like big wages compared to what I had been used to. We thought we were well off, able to buy a few things for the house and so on. Finally I bought out a janitorial business. I have five employees working for me, and my son is in it too.

One thing sticks in my mind about my early life. All that time I had an uncle in Winnipeg—my father's brother. He left England years ago. He was a master engraver and he had his own business 'Wilson's Printing and Engraving' for years until he died. I met his wife several times after his death. She could never understand why father did not send me out to them. They had no children and they would have taught me the business, she said. She was a lovely person.

When she died several years ago, my wife and I went to Winnipeg to settle her estate and to see she was buried by her husband. I guess my father didn't want me to be a burden on anybody—but it sure would have made things different for me.

Rudy Wilson
Chilliwack, B.C.

I was puzzled as to how they found out that I had spent time playing the organ.

The one thing that stands out in my mind about Dr Barnardo's Home in Toronto was the food. I was delighted to receive four slices of bread and jam for supper instead of the usual three I had received in England. I had arrived in Canada around September 22, 1922, and after being in Toronto for about a week we boys were prepared for our departure to the various farmers. I was put on a train to Woodville, Ontario. I knew nothing about my boss other than his name, Mr I. Jamieson.

I arrived at Woodville around one o'clock and the station master was instructed to telephone the farmer to pick me up. I was told his farm was about six miles away and, since it would be some time before he would arrive, I was invited to the station master's house for dinner. This was my first meal in a Canadian home. They had corn on the cob. Not knowing how to eat the stuff, I waited until I saw how my host tackled this type of vegetable. I came to love it.

Finally the farmer arrived in his horse and buggy and my seven-year stint began in an area called 'The Glen' on Lot 2, Concession 14, of Mariposa Township in Victoria County. Practically all the neighbours there were of Scottish descent.

These people I lived with were kind enough to me. I really had no complaints except that they were childless and I had nobody my own age to fraternize with. But after all I was sent there to work and not to play. I was visited regularly by one of Barnardo's field officers who checked to see that I was well treated and cared for. These visits continued until I was about 15 years old. The first year, when I was 12, I was required to complete my grade eight or entrance examination as they called it. This was the sum total of my education at the little red school house. The lack of education has always been uppermost in my mind and was the most disappointing part of my early life.

After I finished school I was expected to do a fair day's work around the farm. We all have leanings towards one thing or another and mine was music. I sang in the choir at the local Presbyterian church. But being brought up in the Church of England I decided I would like to attend that church at Cannington, about eight miles away. I got hold of a bicycle and took off, but I was not used to riding it and the going was rough. I finally arrived at the church, fell off the bicycle with terrific cramps in both legs and, ended up in the ditch. I never did get into the church.

The people for whom I worked were strict and they expected me to follow their instructions. One day before they went to Woodville to shop they told me to hoe the garden, which I did for a while. However, I gave in to a yen to play an old foot-pump organ that was in the parlour. After a while I decided I should complete the hoeing. When they returned I was called into the house and chastised for not working while they were away and warned that any more of these episodes would result in my being returned to the Home. I was puzzled about how they found out that I had played the organ. Then it dawned on me that I had neglected to push the stops in when I had finished playing.

Canada at the time seemed to be a rough country in which to live. However, it built up in one a great initiative to spread out, grow, and be self-sufficient. When one is young, the roughness is borne without question or harm. I recall that for the first two years of my contract I received my board and a small amount of spending money. After two years I was given $20 per month and board for the spring and summer months. In the fall and winter only board was given.

When I became 19, I decided that the farm was no place for me and went to Toronto. In 1929 I started to work at the *Ladies Home Journal* as a pattern cutter for ladies' dresses.

Finally I was married in 1934 and had two boys. I enlisted in the Signal Corps in 1939 and arrived overseas in 1940. This was a big thrill as I had not been back since emigrating in 1922. I visited old friends, and recalled the times we had when I was a boy of 12.

Canada has been good to me and I have to thank Dr Barnardo's Homes for making a complete change in my life. Although I never knew a mother or father, I feel that through the influence of the Home I was able to grow up and be of service to mankind.

James Rook
Newmarket, Ontario

When things get rough, a good soldier never looks behind. He just keeps going.

My mother came with us to Canada. She had to go and scrub floors for doctors and other big people. Many's the time she came home tired out after doing two or three large homes with 50 cents from each of them. My sister Annie was 12 and I was 10 and we had to go out to work on farms. My brother Tom was eight. We were brought out together in 1923 through the Salvation Army.

My first job was with a man called John Wilson at Holloway, Ontario. He had an awful temper but I tried hard to get along with him. I stayed one year. Next I was with a farmer called Clinton Casey on the third concession of Thurlow near Belleville, Ontario. I was up at five o'clock in the morning, milked nine cows, fed the pigs and horses, and cleaned the stables before breakfast. I also worked for Sam Dean in Belleville who treated me like a man and I worked very hard. I got $10 per month but by the time I bought boots, shirts and other things I was broke for another month.

After working for five and one-half years for farmers I had had enough and I came into the city of Belleville. I worked for a Mr Brown in the fish business. After one year I ended up frying fish and chips which was supposed to be an advancement from cleaning fish. Then I went into the business myself. In those days you could buy whitefish for three cents a pound and herring for half a cent a pound. Business was very good. I started out with a hand wagon selling from door to door and within a couple of months I had an old Ford truck. I stayed in this business for five years and did well.

I had a wonderful mother. She would say that when things got rough a good soldier never looks behind. He just keeps going. This stuck with me all my life. I have been in all kinds of businesses. Now I have Robert's Barber Shop and am doing fine. We have six boys and 17 grandchildren.

Robert J. Guthrie
Belleville, Ontario

ELEVEN

THE YEARS
1826–1927

I was a trade union man and took my trade union ideas to Canada.

The first night on the farm at Innerkip, near Woodstock, was lonely. I heard a train whistle blowing and I'd like to have bought a ticket and returned to England. I was 19 years old at the time and had come out on the Montrose in 1927, in care of the Salvation Army. I stayed a year at Innerkip and then went to Littlewood near London, Ontario, for four years. I had a trip back to England during this time and the British Broadcasting Corporation interviewed me and another boy about how we were getting along.

I said that when I had worked in England I was a trade union man and took my union ideas to Canada. I don't believe my Canadian boss had ever heard of a union. I had always imagined that Saturday afternoons off were an Englishman's inherited right.

I guess I was wrong. We worked just as long on Saturdays as any other day and Sundays as well. On one day I remember we were up at five in the morning and worked all day haying. It began to cloud over and there were several loads of hay still to get under cover. By going all out we had every forkful under cover by eight, before the storm broke. After that there was the milking. And yet I was rather pleased about it. I tell you it's wonderful what a chap gets used to.

There was lots of food. If I missed a meal the farmer was more concerned than I was. I was often told that I had to eat to work. But some boys did not 'find their feet'. It depended so much on local conditions and the farmer. You got good and bad farms and farmers.

The other boy on the radio program had been placed near Brandon, Manitoba. He had a contract and a letter of introduction. The farmer said the forms were not worth the paper they were printed on. He would not discuss wages and was generally contemptuous of farm trainees, saying that Britain was merely unloading her unemployed on Canada. This boy said that he worked along with other men who got $5.00 a day for doing the same work that he got paid $25 a month for. His second place was worse. There the farmer told him that if he didn't like it, there were other men to be had from the immigration hall at Winnipeg. So he was put down for deportation for refusing farm work.

On my return to Canada I worked on a farm at Embro near Woodstock, and there I stayed until I enlisted. The wages were paid according to Ontario government orders: $155 and board for the first year, $200 for the second year and $300 from then on. My wages in 1939 were $300 and board.

I married while on service in England and my wife followed me to Canada in 1945. I started as an attendant in the psychiatric hospital in St Thomas and now I am a supervisor. I shall have been here 25 years next August—altogether a very good 42 years as far as I am concerned.

William Coleman
St Thomas, Ontario

I frequently have nightmares about this part of my life. In each case this brute appears and is endeavouring to grab me.

Several years after my mother died in 1914 my youngest sister and I were boarded out to a family in Romney in the south of England. We spent about four years in this town and were treated well. Then my sister went to Dr Barnardo's Girls' Home in Ilford, Essex, and I went to Woodford. A year or so later I was separated from her to come to Canada.

There were about a hundred children from the Home on the Minnedosa. We felt lonely, leaving what friends we had behind. The food was placed before us, and lots of it, but no one felt like eating. When we arrived in Canada we were checked out by a doctor. This doctor hinted that I might live for maybe five years. I was 11 and weighed 75 pounds.

When we were taken to the distribution centre at 538 Jarvis Street, Toronto, we were told that we could ask to be placed near one of the group. I asked, but I never saw any of them again.

I was sent to Port Dalhousie to a fruit farm owned by Mr and Mrs H. Armstrong. They treated me well. They were English and understood how I was feeling. There I became dreadfully sick, gorging myself with fruit I had never seen before. I was supposed to have gone to school, but they never sent me. Shortly after I was back at Jarvis Street. I think it was because I could not do the work required of my small body.

My next assignment was to a place called Pontypool, Ontario, 13 miles north of Newcastle. It was a dairy farm rented by a husband and wife. A strange boy about 14 came there with me. We were allowed to go to school for about six months and then this man took us out of school to work full time on the farm. The wife was kind and gentle, but the husband was unscrupulous, vicious, dirty, and lazy. We were beaten every day or so for the smallest things. The wife would come to our rescue but she would only be cast aside by this crazed being. This man once put my friend on the big stove and held him there until his clothes began to burn. To this day I frequently have nightmares about this part of my life. In each case this brute appears and is endeavouring to grab me. I have a summer cottage about 75 miles north of Pontypool and I sometimes drive past this farm. Something seems to draw me back. These people have gone from there long ago. I did not try to keep track of them.

We boys were visited by a Mr Black about once every three months while we were in this place. He was a kind, solid individual and I am sure he could tell that conditions were not good. We were too scared to divulge anything. That would be sure to get us another beating. Someone must have let Mr Black know the truth because we were whisked away one morning real quick, back to Jarvis Street.

My friend was sent elsewhere—I know not where—and I went to a place called Norwood, Ontario, to a dairy farm owned by Mr and Mrs W. Sanderson. The three or four years I spent there were, for the most part, trouble free. It was while there I became interested in music. I bought a violin and these people encouraged me. I now play 10 instruments.

When I reached the age that I became my own boss, I left and spent that night at the Salvation Army in Toronto. Next morning I went to Oakville—worked on two or three small farms until I married in November 1936. I now work for Gulf Oil in Clarkson—27 years of service.

Walter G. Alway
Oakville, Ontario

I put on my second-best suit. The boss told me to get out of the barn or I would scare the cows.

My troubles started on the ship—the Ascania. I had my wallet stolen out of my pocket. It contained what little money I had and my passport and my railroad ticket from Quebec to Winnipeg. I do not know what arrangements were made by the Church Army who was sponsoring me, but I was passed through customs and boarded the train for Winnipeg. It was the dirtiest train I have ridden on.

Just before we arrived I put on a new grey suit and when we got off at a stop to stretch our legs, one of the boys threw a bunch of oily waste and hit me in the middle of the waistcoat and ruined my suit. So we had a fight on the train which did not go over very big with the officials.

We arrived at Winnipeg on June 22, 1926, and were taken to the hostel on Smith Street. I've forgotten the number on Smith but it was south of Broadway. We all had a good bath and a big supper and felt pretty good again.

The next day was my 15th birthday. I was put on the train for Elkhorn, Manitoba, and hired out to a farmer there for the huge sum of $6.50 per month. We had been told in England that we would get $40 a month. Quite a difference.

When I arrived at the farm I was shown to a shed—I later learned it was a granary—and in it was a pile of straw which was to be my bed, and an old chair. I was then told to put on my work clothes and help with the chores. I did not know what to wear so I put on my second-best suit. The boss told me to get out of the barn or I would scare the cows.

The next morning they got me up at five o'clock to milk. I had never been near a cow in my life before. I had just come from London. What would I know about farming? After breakfast—which I had in the kitchen while the family ate in the dining-room—he took me out to the field with four horses to harrow a field. It was my first day and I was scared.

Several nights later, after the milking, I was carrying a pail of skim milk to feed the pigs. I stopped at the well to pump water for the cows and set down the milk at the edge of the well. Somehow the tail of the long English coat I was wearing got caught on the pail and the milk was dumped into the well. The farmer made me stay at that pump night and day until I was pumping water that was clear of milk. It took me three days.

I was only with these people for three months but it was my start in Canada.

For the past 20 years I have been employed by the Highways Department of the Province of Manitoba. Things have turned out well for me, through hard work and self-education.

Frank Searle
Brandon, Manitoba

Our quota of work was 125 logs a day.

I left Sheffield, England, in the spring of 1926 when I was 15. My sister who is still in Sheffield put up the money, and a fellow by the name of Billy Talbot came out with me on the Cunard ship Alawnia. We landed in Halifax, then went by train to Montreal. There was a hostel across from the Windsor Station from where we were both shipped to a place called Foresters Falls. Bill went to a farmer by the name of Bennets and I to a fellow called Jack Reynolds. The farmers had farms side by side.

I was amazed by this giant country. So free, so much land, and I guess I said to myself 'I love it.' I stayed on the farm for about 14 months. I was treated well and the farm work was a good experience. But I wanted to see more of Canada. If you have ever been to Sheffield you could understand why. It was a dirty city: polluted water, smoke and soot. It was strictly a steel city.

Well, Bill and I went to Pembroke. We got a job selling Fuller brushes. My territory was Eganville. I did O.K. and sold about $100 worth of brushes. I sent the weekly orders in but didn't get any answers from the office in Hamilton. We had to eat, so we took our samples back to Eganville and sold them to the customers, and my share was $75. We never again saw the guy who introduced us to the product.

The fall of 1927 we went to work in a lumber camp at $40 a month. I guess we were the only English-speaking fellows there. We were up on the Black River about 200 miles into Quebec Province from Fort Coulonge. We had to walk for about four days stopping at night and at various eating places. When we got there we all had to build sleeping shacks, a diner and blacksmith shop. They were all comfortable and I really got a thrill out of it. There was lots of food and lots of fresh air.

We would go out in the morning at the break of day with a six-foot saw, and my partner could speak hardly any English. But I learned quite a bit of French. Our quota of work was 125 logs a day. I would lug that six-foot saw on my back with wedges and axe and wade through three and four feet of snow cutting down big pines. After four months of this I felt like a man, muscles bulging like a prize fighter.

Since that time I have seen a lot of the world, but it was that winter in the logging camp that left the big impression. To look out from our camp and see galloping deer on the lake being chased by wolves, and to look down the steep slopes to the fast-flowing Black River with its genuine sweet clear water, with the Laurentian Mountains as far as the eye could see, and the pines whistling in the breeze—that was an experience I'll never forget.

Allan M. Slade
Kingston, Ontario

What would have happened to us waifs if there had been no Homes?

I was raised in England at the Congleton Branch of the National Childrens' Home and came to Canada in August 1926, when I was 16. There were about 30 or 40 boys and girls on the Regina. A Miss Stalker was in charge of us and we had a 'ball'. When we landed in Canada we were taken to the Home at Hamilton, Ontario. I stayed there for about three weeks and was then taken to Maplewood, near Tavistock, Ontario, where I worked for two years for a man called John Bean. The Beans were a good Christian family. I then went to work for a man called Dunsmore who was also very good to me. Really my life as an orphan boy was very good.

It is true that not too many 'Home Children' got an education, but some did go to night school to try to catch up. In those days even boys and girls who had homes and parents did not get much more, because of lack of money and government help. I think we all had about the same chance. When we had a job it was up to us to learn all we could the hard way. Some of us were able to say 'I made it', and that was a good feeling.

Many of the boys were afraid of the unknown. They felt that maybe the first home they had was hard, so ran away in search of love and help. Many who were afraid to run away went close by to some other farmer whom they admired and got him to hire them. This was a new deal for them and they felt more secure. Then they were able to rise above their frustrations and seek friendships in local churches and among the local people. We all faced this problem in the early years of coming out here.

During my life in Canada, I have met Dr Barnardo boys and girls, and most of what I have heard from them is good. Yes, there has been the odd voice of protest, but that is par for the course. Many came to Canada with a chip on their shoulder and at the turn of the century they found life hard. Oh there were heartaches and times when we slept on tearstained pillows, lonesome for the old pals in the Home.

In the Home most of us learned the cardinal rule of self-discipline. This was a great help to us and it is interesting to note that many orphan boys and girls have a low criminal record. We had to face facts with no one to help us. We had to make it on our own. I went through that stage and many boys I know have told me that they did too. Many did not get too much help when they first came out. But what would have happened to us waifs if there had been no Homes? As I look back on all the hard work we did, I feel it has helped us to face the problems that children with parents cannot, and will not, face.

One thing upset me a lot over here. When many of us married, our families wanted us to bury the 'orphan skeleton', and old connections were cut off because of this. But I am proud to be an orphan. I feel I have done well in Canada, that I have become a good citizen and can look back and say I have risen above all the hurts and loneliness of life.

E. Marshall
Toronto, Ontario

I did dishes, churned cream, washed floors, painted, and baby-sat. Just loved every minute of it.

First day on board the Montrose the tables in the dining-room were all full, but several days later when the ship hit the Atlantic only a few were down to meals. A deck hand told me and another boy to get a bottle of Bass and drink it and it would cure our sickness. We had to get somebody older to buy it for us and we each drank half. What awful-tasting stuff! But it really worked and things looked rosy the rest of the trip.

There were 12 boys in our group ranging in age from 14 to 17 years. We left Liverpool on April 19, 1926, and arrived in Canada on April 29—my 16th birthday.

There was boxing on the hatch most afternoons and I won several prizes purchased with the money given by the first-class passengers who watched from the higher decks. One older boy from another group pretty well beat up our older boys—so my group suckered me into taking him on. They didn't know that my brothers were real good boxers and had taught me well. My opponent's friends yelled 'Murder the English bloke' and I remember dropping below his guard and hitting him right on the button. Boy—was I a hero. First time I had ever knocked anyone out.

There was a country-type Swedish girl about 21 years old at our table. At meal times I used to stand and place her chair for her when she came down. At the end of the trip she kissed me and told me in poor English that I was a little gentleman. Boy—was I ever in Heaven because, even with the clothes they wore in those days, you could tell she had class. Even 16-year-old boys have their dreams, eh?

One day I went to have a bath and noticed some small pimples under and around my arms and chest. The man in charge of us looked at them and told me to be quiet about it or they might not let me land. It sure was painful at times but I managed to hang on and went through the customs.

When we arrived at the hostel on Osborne Street in Montreal, Mr Kelly sent me to the doctor who pronounced that it was 'shingles'. I had to dab on stuff every day until I was better, and I stayed in the hostel two weeks longer than the other boys.

When I was healed, Mr Kelly gave me a railroad ticket to a place called Lancaster, in Glengarry County, close to the Quebec border. I had been placed on a dairy farm with the Arnold McPherson family with wages of $10 a month and board. Mrs McPherson was 23 years old and a real gem. I had certainly come to a fine place and I stayed there for two years. Any time we were not busy Arnold would tell me to go to the house and help Jenny. I did dishes, churned cream, washed floors, painted, babysat—and just loved every minute of it. The barn was close to the house and it was wonderful to smell fresh bread and coffee in the morning. The only coffee I had ever seen before was Camp Coffee in a bottle.

It seemed I had picked up some head lice on the boat and I can remember Mrs McPherson turning the old cow clippers while Arnold cut off all my hair. Then they put coal oil on my head. It worked too.

I learned how to milk by hand, drive a team, load manure, stook grain, and load hay with an old hay loader. First time I saw a ground-hog it chased me grinding its teeth. I jumped up on the wagon box and the threshers laughed.

Jenny was in tears the day I left for my next place at Williamsburg, north of Kitchener. Mr Newberry, an Englishman, was my boss there. They had a herd of Jerseys and took cream, eggs, and vegetables to the Kitchener market. This meant getting up at four in the morning on Saturdays so as to have the milking done in time to leave. Every once in a while he would tell me how lucky I was to be eating meals with them, because in England I would be eating in the back kitchen.

From Williamsburg I went to Bloomingdale and worked for the Sheppards, a nice Mennonite family who had a fine dairy herd and lots of pigs. We cut wood in the winter and it was my job to draw it to the Kitchener market and sell it on Saturday. Sometimes I sold seven or eight loads and would deliver it during the week. I stayed there for three years at $360 a year. Things were looking up at last.

My next place was up the road at the farm of Jonas Bingeman and son. They had dual-purpose Shorthorns and milked three times a day. This left me little time for courting and I had met a nice girl from Haysville. I didn't have much money either; wages were down to zero because of the Depression. I even worked just for my board for three months while looking for a job. All I could find that spring was a job for the season, eight months, working on Dr H. W. McLaren's farm at Rutherglen east of North

Bay, Ontario. The farm manager and his wife—Mr and Mrs Haines—were very good to me and the country was just wonderful. Mrs Haines made her own bread which was lovely and we caught fish in a nearby lake in our spare time. We had pike, pickerel, and whitefish all summer. I really hated to leave there in the fall.

I advertised in the paper for a dairy farm job and had a reply from Murray Johnson of Avon, Ontario. This was April 1933 and I stayed there until 1953; at last I had found my niche. Wages were $225 a year for a top man in 1933, and I worked a raise every year until it was $2400 a year when I left. In October 1934 I married Violet Walton, and Mr Johnson moved a house from another farm for us to live in. Being fond of music, I purchased a used C-melody saxophone and had to practise in the barn. This bothered the cows so much I ended playing it in the silo. Several of us formed a little band called the Avon Hot Shots. We played around at garden parties.

After 21 years as herdsman I made up my mind to become an inspector with the federal department of agriculture. I now have 17 years service and hope maybe to retire in 1974.

Colin Perry
London, Ontario

Not only that, but I left behind three sisters whom I have never heard from and cannot seem to get track of.

It was awful hard coming out as a 'Home' boy. They pretty well did what they wanted with you. There was not very much supervision from the Home. If you did something wrong they took you away and sent you to some other place. I came over here in March 1927 and went to the old Marchmont Home in Belleville. I arrived there early in the morning and by afternoon I was on my way to my first place of work—a farm in Prince Edward County. It was a hard place to work. There was no time to play. I got up in the morning at five o'clock, helped with the milking and the rest of the chores. Before I went to school I helped to split wood for the stoves and in the summer on the way to school—which was four miles away—I would take the cows to the pasture and to the creek for water. I walked, in all, about five miles before school and did the same on my way home at night. It was not too easy at times.

I was only there two years when they got another older man. By this time the Marchmont Home had closed down so I was shipped to the

Barnardo Home on Jarvis Street. I went out to another place but could not stand what they had me doing, so I went on my own and never bothered the Home after that.

While I was on these farms I was allowed just 10 cents a week for spending money. That was taken out of the $25 a year that we got for working. You did not get out to play with other boys and girls. It was all work. Not only that but when I came over here I left three sisters behind in England. I have never heard from them and cannot seem to get track of them. Before I left, two of them were in the Sheltering Homes in Liverpool. Their names were Dorothy and Daisy Betts. Another thing—they never sent a birth certificate with me to tell me anything about myself, but when I was in the army in England I went in and got mine and found out that I was born in Hastings, England, in 1913. My wife also came out from England but went to the Barnardo Home in Peterborough. She really had a harder time than I did.

When I went on my own I returned to Prince Edward County and there I met a man and his wife who looked after me and used me like their own. I was with them from the time I was 17 years old and called them Mom and Dad and their two daughters were the same as sisters to me. He worked just the same as I did, and he would not give me a job he would not do himself. He taught me to drive a car and every Saturday they would take me to town with them. Lots of times I would have the car myself. I owe them an awful lot and I miss them very much now that they are gone. I try to make it up by looking after their graves and putting flowers and wreaths out for them. They were wonderful people and I shall never forget them and what they did for me.

Joseph D. Betts
Belleville, Ontario

TWELVE

THE YEARS
1928–1930

I received a rather frosty welcome but they did find me a job.

As a Scottish lad of 14, I left school, fully intending to go to work in one of the woollen factories to help my mother with the household expenses. She was having a hard time living on a war pension. I found a job which was temporary—on and off—for almost three years. Then the Depression closed down most of the factories.

I applied for work at the 'burroo' as the unemployment office was known locally, and while waiting in line to be interviewed I noticed a brochure advertising the Cossar Farm for boys wishing to emigrate to Canada, Australia, or New Zealand. You see, Mr G.C. Cossar of Glasgow, had farms in each of these countries.

I was duly accepted at the Cossar Farms in Craigielin near Paisley, Scotland, where I spent a period of five weeks or so in training. Some of the boys, including myself, were loaned or hired out—I am not sure which—to some of the local farmers. The Craigielin Farm had 40 boys in training, and a group left every week from Greenock for Canada or Australia.

This farm was run on very strict, almost military lines and the superintendent was a bit sadistic. I witnessed this on two occasions. It was the custom at bedtime to line up in the hall and do a hundred stretch-and-touch-toes exercises. After this it was to bed with the lights out at 9:30. On two occasions the whistle was blown at 10:30 p.m. and the Captain called out the names of a number of boys who had neglected to check their tools into the warehouse after work. These boys were ordered downstairs and up the hill to the back fields—in some cases half a mile away—to pick up their

166

tools. Anyone who has been in Scotland in early spring would know how bitter cold it would be outside in a nightshirt and bare feet. As the boys descended the stairs, the superintendent, his wife, and the kitchen help were on hand, giggling and laughing at the embarrassment of the boys. Some of them had on extremely short nightshirts; this was to the advantage of the superintendent who administered a heavy stroke with a leather strap as each boy turned at the bottom of the stairs. Needless to say there were no tools forgotten for a few days.

On my arrival at Gagetown, New Brunswick, in May 1929 I had to remain at the Cossar Farm for five days. I had been vaccinated for chicken pox on board the Andania and my arm was healing. At this time, there was an orchard of 6,000 fruit trees on the Cossar farm, and it was stocked with Yorkshire pigs, Clydesdale horses, and dual-purpose Shorthorn cattle. A local boy was in charge of the barns and the Cossar boys helped him. I received my room and board while I was there.

My first posting was to the farm of Mr A. S. Orchard at Young's Cove on Grand Lake, New Brunswick. I remained there for three years. My wages were my room and board, plus $12 per month the first year, and $15 per month for the second and third years. Out of this I was supposed to clothe myself and pay $40 to the Cossar Farm. During my first month with the Orchards I was kicked in the head by a horse and spent some time in the hospital at Saint John. I was expected to pay my hospital expenses.

When the Orchards moved away from the farm I returned to the Cossar Farm to get help in locating a new job. I received a rather frosty welcome, but they did find me a job in Hampton, New Brunswick, at the fabulous wage of $1.00 per day and board.

The day started at four in the morning with the help staggering out to the barn to begin the chores—milking 100 cows by hand. The barn work was usually done by six o'clock and breakfast was at seven. After breakfast we went down to the slaughter house to kill two or three head of beef or pork whichever happened to be on order from the local stores. The help would be fortunate to be in bed by 10 at night.

Two bright spots stand out in my memory of this farm: the food was good and we attended church services on Sunday at the Anglican Church in the village. The farmer was an ardent churchgoer and his voice could be heard loud and clear during the singing of the hymns.

I spent four or five years on this farm. Then I got discouraged and decided to go back to Scotland. I worked my way over on a cattle boat from Saint John. I had to pay $15 hush money to the agent at Saint John in order to get my name on the list. I discovered the Depression was still in full swing in Scotland, so after a short stay I returned to Hampton for a few years, and then drifted to the coal fields of the Chipman area. I have lived and worked here ever since.

I think the Cossar boys were looked upon as a source of cheap labour, and maybe they were resented in some areas. But a good many remained in Canada and fared quite well.

William Donaldson
Chipman, New Brunswick

I was cursed like a slave not knowing what to do to please and I tried so hard.

I didn't have to come out here in the first place, for I had a good job as rivet boy at the age of 16. I started to work at the Chatham Dock Yard, Admiralty Ship Building, Kent, England, in 1926 and worked there until June 1929.

As a boy I was quite religious. In Chatham where I lived, my place of worship was St Paul's Church. I had from time to time spoken to my minister about going to another country to preach. He said my education wasn't good enough. The reason for my poor education was that my mother was a war pensioner; my father was in World War I and got killed in 1918 on Armistice Day. She had to go out and work, and lots of times she was sick so I lost a lot of school days, being the older of two boys. We had three sisters who died earlier with the flu. Well, the minister's helper (I forget what we called him) encouraged me to emigrate, which seemed fun to me at 18, but my mother was upset. Her last words were: 'You'll be sorry', and for the first 10 years I was good and sorry.

We sailed from Southampton on June 14, 1929, on the Montcalm. I had my birthday on the boat 19 years old, four days out on the ocean. I am not too sure how long it took us to get to Montreal, probably 10 days. We went through immigration all right and got on a train which took us to Indian Head, Saskatchewan. There were quite a lot of boys from England to Montreal but as we went across Canada the boys got off at different stations. Some of the boys got off at Indian Head where we went to a hostel and stayed about four days. It's a funny thing, as I think back to those four days, it seems we ate nothing but porridge and macaroni. I don't think I minded it. I was grateful for it. It's just that it has struck me these last few years, since then I've hated macaroni and porridge. I don't know why. They seemed to have tasted all right at the time.

Around July 1, 1929, a representative came and took me to a farm 14 miles from Whitewood, Saskatchewan, where we met a farmer and his wife. The man from the Church of England explained why I was there. He said I was to work for three years at $10 a month. At the end of that time, if I'd saved up $300, the Church of England (or the government I am not too sure which) would put the rest to it and start me up on a homestead. I was agreeable and so were the farmer and his wife. I think it was on a Saturday. On Sunday I got acquainted. Monday morning about six o'clock I went downstairs ready for work (I was used to getting up early, as I thought, in England). The whole family, including two small boys, were eating breakfast.

'Good Morning' I said.

Then the farmer said 'Good Morning' with a question mark. 'We have been up since four o'clock' he said 'and milked 28 head of cattle and slopped the pigs and nearly finished our breakfast.'

Well, that not only spoiled my breakfast, but three years to come. Can you imagine me—a boy, 5 ft 3 in, about 120 pounds, who had never been on a farm in his life—feeding, milking by hand 28 cows, bringing them up to the barn at four o'clock every morning from the bush, besides currying six Clydesdale horses, putting harness on same and feeding and slopping the hogs which they had, from 25 to 50 of, all the time? I had to make sure there was wood in the house, separate the milk from the cream, make butter, go out in the field, plough and harrow, stook the grain, and get beat once or twice a day if I didn't keep my end up. The only thing I didn't do, was go out in the field on a Sunday. It took me all day Sunday to look after the other things I have mentioned.

I went to the village of Whitewood three times in three years. I scarcely ever left the farm. On Saturday I would hurry and get the work done and after the farmer and his family went to town I would wander across the field. I thought it was wonderful to see the lovely trees and birds and rabbits. It was just like being born again. I walked for miles all alone and it used to take my mind off things. Although there were times when I was so lonely I sat down and cried. I hadn't known what it was like until then not to be loved. I was cursed like a slave not knowing what to do to please and I tried so hard.

Well, as I walked I came upon a small farm just starting up like a homestead. The trees and bushes were all round the buildings. I watched from a distance of about 200 or 300 yards and saw children running around and a man and woman fixing the house. I tried to keep out of sight but the children saw me and ran over. We looked at one another until I spoke to them but I couldn't understand them, nor they me. Then the biggest boy' About 10 or 12 years old, got hold of my hand and wanted me to go with them. They took me to their father and mother but I couldn't understand them. I found out they were Hungarians. They turned out to be wonderful friends and I had some meals there. We tried to teach one another.

They used to call me Ge-me for Jimmy. The farmer didn't like me visiting the Hungarians because they weren't English. But I used to go and not tell him.

I was bound and bent that I was going to save up all I could so that I could write and tell my mother that I had made it. The farmer bought me a few clothes now and then—nothing to write home about. My hair was long like a hippie's. I did not ask for any money at all. Every September after the crops were all right they would go on a two-week vacation to Brandon, Manitoba—the four of them and leave me to look after everything. There is more to this than meets the eye, but it is very hard for me to put it in writing. I damn near froze to death sleeping at the top of the two-storey frame house. There was no stove except downstairs where they all slept. When I complained they said that I was lucky, that other farmers put their hired help in the barn, and because I said I would rather sleep in the barn they gave me a hiding that I'll never forget. One time I went to the Church of England minister in Whitewood while they were away on their vacation and told him everything. He wouldn't believe me. He also told the family. I got another licking.

Well, time went on. Then came July 1932. All that month I kept talking (off and on) about my wages. I figured I'd earned $360 minus $20 which I'd spent. As you may know, $1.00 was worth $10 by today's standards, or thereabouts. Well, he kept putting me off. He wouldn't say too much about it. July and August went by; then came September and no sign of my being paid for my three years' work and knocking around. The second week in September came. The farmer and his wife told me at the dinner table that they were going on another two-week vacation to Brandon, and that they would settle up with me when they came back. I thought two weeks wouldn't hurt me so I went along with it. I thought the end of that two weeks would never come. After waiting for three years and three months, I should have $390 less $20—$370. They were back a week and didn't say anything so I brought it up and he told me that he couldn't pay me but he would give me a piece of land that was next to the house. I wish you could have seen that land.

Nothing but rock and sow thistle. It had never been worked and never would be. I would have had to clear it myself. With what? I had no money to buy equipment. I didn't like it at all, but I told him I would think it over. I wanted to homestead, but on my own with the help of the Church of England.

On a Saturday, I asked for a day off which I got, but I had to walk the 14 miles to Whitewood. They had a model A Ford but I never rode in it. Well, I got a ride with a farmer and I spoke to him about it and he said 'You won't get your money and as far as the piece of land goes—he can't give it to you.'

I asked him 'Why not?'

'Because the land doesn't belong to him in the first place. He's a returned soldier from England (which I knew) and the land belongs to the Soldiers' Settlement which makes him a homesteader and he is still paying the government. Everything he owns belongs to the government.'

So where did that leave me? Holding the bag. I went on to town and I went into the Mounted Police office and asked them what I could do and they told me the same as the farmer. They also told me to go to the Church of England—the head office in Toronto. Well, that took the life right out of me. What could I do with no money? I went to the church again but I might just as well have stayed away.

Eventually I went back to the farmer and told him everything I had learned and he admitted it.

'Why didn't you give me my money instead of going on that vacation?' I asked.

He had no answer. I told him that I was leaving Monday. He said I couldn't leave until I had notified the church. He was trying to stall me so I would stay. He even offered me $15 a month. I said 'How can you pay me $15 when you couldn't pay me $10?' He had no answer for that either. So I told him I was going to Toronto to the head office and I would like $50 to get there, but he said he didn't have it. I left with nothing on Monday. This was the end of September 1932.

Can anybody realize what I went through in my mind after three years and three months? They didn't even offer to drive me into town so I started to walk, baggage and all. Well, I must say I didn't have to walk very long. Another farmer came along and gave me a ride to Whitewood. By this time my experiences had really got around. This farmer who was giving me the ride knew everything. When I told him that I was going to try to get to

Toronto he said 'Why don't you get another job. You'll never get there before winter comes with no money in your pocket.' He said that he could get me a job for the winter and then in the spring I could still go east if I wanted to. So I decided to stay. He took me to another farm that was owned by friends of his—a Mr and Mrs W. Anderson. After meeting them, they said they would like to have me but they couldn't pay me too much for the winter as things were getting quite bad. I will admit that times were getting bad in 1932.

I accepted the job and I can't speak highly enough of these people. It was just like home away from home, so to speak. Everywhere they went in their car, they took me—to dances and house parties. I met more people in those few months than I did in the three years with the other farmer. They thought of me as their own son, and as far as I was concerned, they were like a mother and father to me. I had pocket money all the time; not too much but enough for my own use. The food was a lot better than at the other place. I had a lovely room to sleep in and more comfortable too. I had the run of the whole house which I didn't have before. On the other farm I couldn't go into the front room to listen to the radio. I had to stay in the kitchen or go up to my cold small room. At the Andersons I could do anything and they told me to make myself at home. Not only that, they took me to church, which I had missed very much.

I made the mistake of leaving there in the spring of 1933 and going down to Toronto to the Church of England headquarters to see about my pay. I had quite a session there. They said they couldn't help me. They also said I should have stayed on the farm, for at least I had a roof over my head. They said times were bad in Canada. Then I asked them to deport me back to England, but they said they couldn't unless I killed someone. A nice thing to say, and coming from the Church of England too.

I started to look for a job in Toronto, no matter how small. I had no money and no place to go. On my travels I spoke to a big, friendly Negro. I asked him about work. He smiled and said 'Join the gang' and shook hands with me. I forget the name of the place where he took me. It was a big building and there were crowds of people outside waiting to get in. Probably it was the Salvation Army. I stayed there for two days trying to get a job but no luck. I walked out, thumbed my way from Toronto to Trenton, Ontario. Then I worked at different farms, highway jobs, canning factories and cotton mills. I had three years at the Trenton Airport, 20 cents a day and board. Then on to Kingston to Vimy Barracks. In 1939 I joined the Army but was discharged as not physically fit to go overseas.

Finally in 1948 I started at Dupont of Canada, and I've been there for 21 years. I am now happily married and have six children and ten grand-children.

James J. Crookes
Kingston, Ontario

I was walking down Yonge Street and looked in a window of a store that was selling kids' toys. It occurred to me that I could make far better ones.

My most vivid memory as an orphan boy in the Quarrier Homes goes back to the day I first held a tanner, a six-penny piece, in my hand. I found it and I had a great dream about how I would spend it. I wanted a ball. Oh, there were lots of balls and other sports equipment at the school, but I wanted a ball that was just mine. I asked the teacher to buy it for me in the village, and she told the principal. Well, the principal thought I had stolen the money and when I wouldn't say I had, I was sent to a man named Mooney to make me confess that I hadn't found it. I was wearing short pants and I got a real strapping, but I stubbornly stuck with the truth. Blood was running down the back of my legs when I returned to class. Teacher asked me a question and I didn't stand up to answer. The backs of my knees were so sore I was afraid to move—afraid if I did I would break down and cry and that would have hurt my pride. She came down and pulled me to my feet. When she found out what had happened she went to the principal and handed in her resignation.

I was placed in the Home in 1918, after both of my parents died of the flu. I was a keen scholar. When I asked to be sent to Canada at the age of 16, the principal tried to persuade me to stay in Scotland and finish my education. But adventure called and in 1928 I was on a ship sailing for Canada. For the first five years I worked as a farm apprentice. This experience confirmed that farming was not for me. When I struck out on my own, Canada was well into the Depression. I bought my first job in the upholstery business and when my money was gone, so was the job. I tried delivering hand bills, and then went back to the farm for a spell. I wanted to be a surgeon. I could do anything with my hands. But instead I went to work for General Motors. Generous Motors, I call them. They put me through an engineering course.

Then came the war. I joined the Air Force and got my pilot's licence. When I came back at the end of the war, I was walking down Yonge Street in Toronto, and looked in the window of a store that was selling kids' toys. It occurred to me that I could make far better ones. I remembered a wagon that my father made for me before he died. I used it as a model for the ones I made. That wagon sold well, but I didn't stay in the toy business. I started designing tools and today I have a firm with 100 skilled machinists. We work 24 hours daily, manufacturing precision instruments and aircraft components.

Meticulousness—that's what the Homes taught me. I designed instruments with meticulousness and they were what set me on the road to success.

W.R. Elliott
Kitchener, Ontario

Back in the 30s the average English immigrant was more despised than pitied.

Looking back on my experiences, out of the gist of it all, I know that an English immigrant today would fare much better due to television and people like the Beatles and the image of swinging old London'. Back in the 30s the average English immigrant was more despised than pitied which did not do us any great harm. In fact I think it gave us the understanding to be more tolerant towards our fellow human beings.

I came to Canada in 1930 under the benevolence of the Crusade of Rescue, and was placed in the care of the Sisters of Charity who were located on Wellington Street, Ottawa. The kindly nuns distributed us out to hard-luck farmers who couldn't afford anyone else. The standard agreement was $5.00 per month and board. We weren't very popular.

My wife and I have successfully adopted and raised two children. The teachings of the nuns and my past experiences have been a great help through the years.

L. Brannigan
Niagara-on-the-Lake, Ontario

The people were nice, but if they had company I would have to eat in the kitchen.

To begin with, a chum and I were walking around in downtown Liverpool and we saw a sign which read, 'Boys wanted to go to Canada, Apply Dr Barnardo's Home.' My mother and father were both dead and I was living with my sister. We went to the Home and they gave us a form for our guardians to sign. My sister signed mine and I was taken into the Home.

I was there for about six months. Once a week we would go to a farm and they would show us how to milk. There was a wooden saw-horse and a rubber bag like a cow's udder, filled with water. That is how we learned to milk. They were the most enjoyable six months of my life. The people at Dr Barnardo's were really good to all of us.

We landed at Quebec City on April 14, 1928, and were in quarantine for two or three days. From there we went to Dr Barnardo's Home on Jarvis Street, Toronto, where I met Mr and Mrs Hobday. I have never known such wonderful people. They were just like a mother and father to us. Words cannot express my feelings for them both.

I was 17 years of age when I was placed on a farm around London, Ontario. The people were nice, but if they had company I would have to eat in the kitchen. I was not good enough to be in the dining room. The wages were $100 a year. I wore the same clothes for about two years. I had a pair of knickers with the long stockings and a shirt with the wide Eton collar. Every Sunday I walked about three miles to church. The inspector from Dr Barnardo's Home came about every two or three months. He would ask me how everything was going. Of course I was only a kid and scared. I did not say much.

I stayed on the farm for about four years but I was homesick so they gave me some money to go to Toronto. I told Mr Hobday that I wanted to go back to England. Again he was very understanding. He talked to me and told me he had a very nice couple who wanted a boy. He also gave me what money I had coming from the other place.

I went to Ripley, Ontario. They were a nice young couple with no children. I stayed with them about three and a half years. While in Ripley I was president of the Anglican Young Peoples' Association and the choir leader. When I left Ripley I got a job on the railroad with the extra gang in the cook car. We were stationed in Welland. There I met my wife and we were married in 1940. We have five children, three of them married.

Thomas Hilton
Welland, Ontario

Talk about pleasant memories.

We were World War I orphans. I was born in Navin, Scotland, November 1912, and my sister Jessie was born in April 1914. I remember neither my mother nor father, only foster parents. My sister was sent to a home near Edinburgh at age 12. I stayed with foster parents until leaving school at 14 and working out. A year later the 'powers that be' wished to know what I wanted to do with my life—go back to school or learn a trade. Either way was recommended.

'Not me' I said. I wanted to go to Australia—as far away as I could get from the kind of life I'd had as a foster child.

Australia I guess wasn't intended to be part of my future. Peter McLean, a school buddy in more or less the same circumstances as myself, was coming with me. We had to pass an examination by our home town doctor. Peter had a bad throat. Dr Wilson said,

'Too long a journey to Australia for you, young man. You can go as far as Canada.'

Peter looked at me and I said 'OK. Canada.'

I wasn't particularly worried about which country it was. We were sent down to a large Salvation Army Home in Hadleigh, Essex, England, for six weeks of training. A toughening-up course really. Peter developed quinsy and didn't sail until two weeks after me. In February 1929 about 400 or 500 of us boys, ages 14 to 19, Scots, English, Irish, Welsh, sailed on the Newfoundland bound for Canada.

After two weeks on the Atlantic our first stop was St John's, Newfoundland. They had just had a big snowstorm and, no kidding, the snow was piled up to the bedroom windows. We were told to get off the boat and to walk to the Salvation Army Citadel. On our way the men shovelling the snow asked,

'Are you kids going west?'

'Yes' we said.

'Oh, it is a lot worse than this out there in Canada.'

We arrived at the Citadel, and talk about pleasant memories! The people of St John's came from every corner of the city and they brought cakes, pies, and all the things boys like to eat. They gave us a real welcome, asked us what part of this country and that country we came from. We played games and sang songs until it was time to get on the boat again for Halifax.

From there we were split into two groups. Half of us were sent to Woodstock, Ontario, and the other half—which included me—were sent to Smiths Falls, Ontario. We stayed at the Salvation Army Home for a few days and then we were sent out to farmers who had their names down for a boy. I was sent to a farmer four miles from Athens, Ontario; he was to pay me $10 a month and give me board. The hours were long and the work was hard but I had a good room and plenty to eat. I was allowed 50 cents a week for pocket money. The balance of the wages was sent to the Home to be put in our account.

When I was about 18 years old I wanted my savings out. The Salvation Army said 'No, not until you are 21.' I heard from some of the boys that you could get your money if you made a trip to the Old Country, so I did this. I had enough for one way and the second farmer I worked for said he would pay my way back and I could work it out later. I stayed three weeks visiting my sister. On the way back I was short of money and nearly didn't make it past the customs in Halifax. After some phone calls I was put back on the boat—Duchess of Atholl—and was the lone passenger to dock at Saint John. From there I went by train to Brockville, to the farmer who had paid my way back. I stayed until my debt was paid.

I was free at last—and not quite 20 years old. I enjoyed life on the farms, played an accordion at parties and travelled around. One year I hitchhiked from coast to coast and saw as much as I could of this great country. I worked now and then on farms to keep myself in pocket money. I was still single and kept on working in lumber camps and on farms until the war.

In 1941 I joined the Canadian Army and served in England and Northwest Europe. Now I am happily married with a family of three, but that is another story.

Robert MacDonald
Dunnville, Ontario

We boys and girls spent weary hours on our knees, scrubbing and waxing miles of wooden hallways.

In 1928 the city of Liverpool, England, held nothing for a 14-year-old boy who had no prospects of learning a trade and who was deficient in education. I had been awarded a Grammar School scholarship, but was too poor to take advantage of it. My widowed mother had four children including myself and in those days a 14-year-old was expected to finish school and begin contributing to the family finances. What to do when there was no job? Emigrate, of course. Canada and Australia were screaming for immigrants.

I chose Canada because it seemed closer. Then my mother had to be won over. At first, she had great doubts about my sanity but finally she relented and said I could go. A Catholic organization in Liverpool assisted me to get to Canada, on condition that I repay them over a stated period of time. So in June of 1928 I found myself an unwelcome resident of St George's Home on Wellington Street in Ottawa. It was there that I became fully aware of how Oliver Twist felt in Dickens' orphanage. The nuns in charge of the Home were tough. We boys and girls spent weary hours on our knees, scrubbing and waxing miles of wooden hallways. Then to prevent any circulation of the blood back to our knees there were innumerable periods of prayer. The nuns thought the desire for food was a mere animal lust and kept this temptation to a minimum.

I began to plot to escape but before I could complete my plans I was banished into the Gatineau, placed with a family who had 150 acres of rocks near Low. I grew to love this family and I know this feeling was reciprocated. To this day we keep in touch even though years and distance separate us.

As time went by I became aware that my contract was not being fulfilled to some extent, but I was happy with the family. I was supposed to get the princely sum of $8.00 a month (to be paid to the Home) and be warmly dressed and well fed. The latter two items were well lived up to, but as the Depression deepened, money became a four-letter word on this farm. Once a year a sad little Catholic priest would stumble in on us, ostensibly to see about my welfare but more to inquire about the lack of the green stuff being forwarded to the Home.

In winter, I drifted up to the bush camps north of Maniwaki. I worked as a logger and often stayed on into the spring. I did a great deal of reading even in the bush camps, and over the years developed into a pretty good cartoonist. After about 10 years I decided to strike farther afield. I rode box cars out west via Sudbury and Timmins, working here and there. While I was harvesting near Saskatoon, World War II broke out and I immediately enlisted in the Canadian Artillery. I wore the uniform for six years. While in England I married a girl from Sussex, and she came to Canada in 1946. I studied for three years at the University of Saskatchewan to become a registered psychiatric nurse, and settled in North Battleford. I like this spot for its location in the parklands and its proximity to the lakes and forest region.

In 1967 the Secretary of State awarded me the Canadian Centennial Medal for 22 years of meritorious service as a psychiatric nurse. I believe I was the only psychiatric nurse in Canada to be so honoured.

A. O'Hanlon
North Battleford, Saskatchewan

I was lucky. The farmer I was sent to was one of the nicest, and poorest, people I have ever met.

I left school at age 13 for purely financial reasons—with five marks out of eight between 90 per cent and 98 per cent it wasn't stupidity.

I got a job in a grocery store. Then started to serve an apprenticeship as a template maker in a large steel firm. Apprentices took a lot of abuse—like being punched by two grown men. I was a boy—a small boy—112 lbs. of runt—and determined to retaliate—which made it worse. I was often black and blue. Of course, I was at fault! I couldn't see the joke when my only pair of boots were filled with glue and a five-inch nail was used to nail them to the floor. It cost a week's wages to pay for those boots and my widowed mother was kind of short of money.

Monday morning at eight o'clock on March 25, 1929, John, one of the apprentices, came to work smiling.

'Going to Australia through the Big Brother Movement' he said. 'Getting out of this hell hole.' At noon I rushed my lunch, got on my bicycle, went uptown and visited Mackey Bros Travel Agency.

'We have nothing for Australia but on Wednesday afternoon you can be interviewed by Canadians.'

Wednesday—interviewed, given a physical, given 35 shillings for clothing. Thursday—bought 'farm' clothes, suitcase. Friday at nine in the morning I was at Waverley Station to Glasgow to Greenock. That evening boarded the Duchess of Bedford lying at anchor in the mouth of the Clyde. The engines started and everyone rushed on deck and bid a fond farewell to Bonnie Scotland. One English boy and 50 Scots were in the group. Monday morning to Friday at eight in the evening. It still surprises me.

One other lad and I, plus our escort, were all who ate breakfast next morning. I never missed a meal. One boy never ate a meal on the whole trip except the Friday supper. If the ship had sunk he would have been happy. The second or third day out the smell below decks was horrible—not really the vomit but the disinfectants. However, as long as I could remain on deck I was fine. But I was always thankful to get away from my cabin which was away, away down. My mother was a good cook—I thought—but the meals on board were fit for a king! I never saw such variety.

One week later we anchored off Saint John. No pier? Just piles driven into the water and a few loose planks on top, three feet wide, to take us to dry land. Later I heard that a fire had swept the waterfront. We wandered around amazed at the snow, in piles seven feet deep, and houses on poles (those are houses? people live there? and it is too late to go back!) The next day, Saturday, at three in the afternoon we were on the train for Toronto but were rerouted through the United States because of a track washout. We arrived on Sunday night where three buses took us to a farm at Norval, Ontario. It was dark; I remember nothing.

We stayed at Norval until Wednesday when we all separately went to different farmers. I only kept track of one of the boys—and he moved from farm to farm for three years, then returned to Scotland.

I was very lucky. The farmer I was sent to was one of the nicest, and poorest, people I have ever met. Mr and Mrs Milton Clements of Milton in Halton County, Ontario, treated me as one of the family. I was chided and I got the occasional pat on the back—both always carefully and with restraint. I only worked one year with them but they never missed a year, from then until they retired from the farm, sending me an invitation to spend Christmas with them. I only once did. Mostly I found myself working Christmas Day.

'Remember you're a Clements', Mrs Clements told me once. 'Oh yes, I know you are a Drummond, but you are one of our family.'

On Mrs Clements' 80th birthday I was invited to the Clements reunion—six sons and four daughters and their families, and a former hired boy, me, Jimmy Drummond, their 11th child, with his family. Mrs Clements died that year.

The depression years were far from nice. I was never out of work for more than one week at a time. On one occasion I held two part-time jobs until one became full time. But wages were small. Once for a year I got $7.00 a week which paid room and food and my savings went down. I washed dishes at the Royal York Hotel in Toronto for 25 cents an hour—wished the job was steady, not just during a convention. Washed windows at the National Club on Bay Street—tried to get on steady—no vacancies. Washed floors at Mt Sinai Hospital, tried to get on steady—got lucky and made it.

While working at Mt Sinai, I spent three nights a week at night school for two years and studied the other nights—$10 per month fees, plus books out of a $40 per month salary (had meals at hospital). Through the kindness of a Miss Rothery I went in training as a nurse and three years later graduated. The marks I made in all three years and in the finals, did, I think, express my thanks for the faith she put in me.

Joined Royal Canadian Air Force in 1942 and did conspicuously nothing for four years. Oh, I obeyed orders—was overseas but never saw a German or Japanese. Only time 'wounded' was parachute jumping indoors in a gym. Was discharged—nursed for a few months—bought a farm and got married. I'm still farming, have a new house, added on adjoining 100 acres for 200 total. Added three sons.

Thank goodness for the three sons. At 56 with arthritis and using a crutch to walk—well, I'd like to retire. But it is not easy. All our money is in land, buildings and machinery—and stock. So I still manage the farm. The boys do the work.

Am I glad I came? One has to experience loneliness to evaluate it. I was lonely. I had no normal youth, no high school days, or friends, or dances. Fortunately, I always loved work. And I made some real good friends (but few friends in total). The Clements' family—the sons and daughters visit us and we visit them and we correspond. If I had not come to Canada—what then? You only go through life once—I'll never know. I've made many mistakes in life—but coming to Canada was not one of them. Mother is now dead. My brothers and sisters softly suggest it was a hasty mistake. I—with a smile—agree only that it sure was hasty.

James Drummond
Kippen, Ontario

Room and board: a blanket in a tent and rabbit stew or goulash every day.

My first job in Canada was collecting sap to make maple syrup on a farm at Lansdowne, Ontario. Wages were $16 per month in the summer and $10 in the winter. The following year my wages jumped to $20 in the summer, but I quit in the fall when the farmer wanted me to work the winter months for just room and board. I was then 16 years old, out from the Quarrier Homes in Scotland in 1930. I didn't know much about the Depression yet.

With one suitcase, I headed for the mine at Kirkland Lake. No job there—moved to Noranda, trying all the mines en route, but no luck. Then to Amos, Quebec, and down to Val d'Or where I tried to get a job at the Lamacque Mines which were just developing at that time—no dice. I ended up burning tree stumps on the side of the new road being opened. My wages were my room and board: a blanket in a tent and rabbit stew or goulash every day.

I backtracked from there to Siscoe Gold Mine which is on an island, and managed to find a bunk in one of the bunkhouses. Eating was a problem here—only one place to get it—in the mess hall. I got kicked out twice, since the stewards knew that I was not an employee. However, after much persuasion a friendly miner captain of Scottish descent gave me a job and I stayed on for a year. Being on an island, there was nothing to do on time off but play cards or pool. After the year I went to Noranda and got a job in the mine. On my first physical I flunked the eye examination. I managed to get a copy of the eye-testing chart, memorized it and applied for work again under the name of Campbell. The result—I passed with flying colours and worked there for a year. I didn't enjoy my stay. The fumes from the smelter would drive you nuts. On top of that, the dirt got into my pores so that after shaving it looked as though I was wearing a black collar.

I quit there and went on to Timmins and got a job at McIntyre Mines. How I managed that I don't know. There were around 200 to 300 men at the gatehouse every day looking for work. Most of my time at the McIntyre was spent in the deep—between the 4,000-foot and 5,500-foot levels and all we wore were a pair of pants and boots. It is hot at that depth. Timmins was a good place to work and there were lots of recreational activities: baseball, miniature golf, a large community centre with a curling rink, hockey rink, bowling alley, auditorium and—best of all—a game room where we could play bridge to our heart's content.

On January 1, 1940, I married the daughter of the woman who ran the boarding house where I was staying. What a way to start the New Year! It was the best thing I ever did. Everything I have now is attributable to her. I really mean that. If it hadn't been for her, I might still have been a miner.

With the war on, I joined the army and served over four years as a wireless technician. After my discharge I came to Cornwall where my wife was teaching and got a job at the Howard Smith Paper Mills. When my wife finished her term teaching we went house-hunting and ended up buying a half acre of land on what was then the outskirts of town, but is now the best residential area. We built our home under the Veterans' Lands Act. Needless to say my wife was the instigator of this.

We raised a family: two boys and two girls. They had it a lot easier than I did when I was their age. However, that is life. One always wants to give his children more than what one had when one was young. They are grown up now, and my wife went into real estate and was doing so well that I quit the mill and became the office manager. So that roughly is my story.

John Cameron

SELECTED INDEX
HOMES

PEOPLE

PLACES

SHIPS

SUBJECTS